A MIGHTY HARD ROAD
THE WOODY GUTHRIE STORY

A MIGHTY HARD ROAD

THE WOODY GUTHRIE STORY

BY HENRIETTA YURCHENCO

ASSISTED BY MARJORIE GUTHRIE
INTRODUCTION BY ARLO GUTHRIE

McGRAW-HILL BOOK COMPANY

New York · St. Louis · San Francisco · Dusseldorf
London · Mexico · Panama · Sydney · Toronto

We are grateful to E. P. Dutton & Co., Inc. for the quote on pages 24–25 from the book BOUND FOR GLORY by Woody Guthrie. Copyright, 1943, by E. P. Dutton & Co., Inc. and reprinted with their permission.

We are grateful to Bob Dylan for permission to include his *Song to Woody* on page 154.

In memory of my father and mother,
Edward and Rebecca Weiss,
who lived through it too.

Library of Congress Catalog Card Number: 73-110963

1234567890 VBVB 7876543210

Book design by James E Barry

Contents

Introduction

Woodys MUSICAL TRAINING came from the songs he heard as a kid. Songs about the people who lived before him. Songs about outlaws and lovers and about everything else that was going down when they were written. So, when he wrote his own songs, he wrote about his friends and neighbors and people he had heard of. That's what most of the good and beautiful and sad and all of the songs we hear on the radio are all about.

When you hear The Beatles or Bob Dylan you know that they're talking about US! Where they get the words and ideas, they use to write these songs is something they might not even know. Woody said they came from YOU!

Arlo

Acknowledgment

I WISH TO ACKNOWLEDGE my gratitude to Mrs. Marjorie Guthrie, without whose loving cooperation in supplying me with materials from the Guthrie files, and her own impassioned personal recollections, this book could never have become a reality.

I am also deeply indebted to my husband, Irving Levine, for his patience and penetrating advice. To Marion Gutmann, my affectionate appreciation for her good sense, skill, and warm devotion in preparing the manuscript in its final form.

Among the numerous others who assisted in many ways, I wish especially to thank Hally Wood Stephensen, Pete Seeger, and Gordon Freisen for pertinent material, Bruce Manheim for help on the songs, and Harold Leventhal of the Guthrie Children's Trust Fund, for many kindnesses extended to me.

Publisher's Note:

WOODY GUTHRIE HAD HIS OWN WAY of seeing things and talking about them. His language was informal, his spelling often unorthodox, but there was always a reason behind his seeming casualness. In quoting various selections from Woody's writings, the publisher has thought it best to present them exactly as they appeared, without changes.

Foreword

I FIRST MET WOODY GUTHRIE one evening in 1940 at the studio of WNYC, New York City's radio station, where I was a producer of special music events. We had just finished a broadcast of folk songs from Kentucky. The telephones were ringing—people calling us from every part of the city, telling us what a good show it had been.

The performers were traditional singers, born and bred Kentuckians, who knew the very smell of the earth and the exact shade of blue of the sky under which they and their British ancestors had lived for generations. That night they had sung about their own troubled Harlan County, of the years-long coal miners' strike, of the fight to organize a union. The words they spoke and the songs they sang recalled poignantly, and with some bitterness, the violence of company thugs, the starvation, and the determination to win a better life. Aunt Molly Jackson, her sister Sarah Ogan, and her half brother Jim Garland, all of them militant strike leaders, were in the studio. And there were others, come to help out.

There was much hubbub in Studio D, guests and performers talking among themselves. Someone touched me on the shoulder. "See that little guy over there, in Levis and a plaid shirt, the one with the wiry-looking hair? That's Woody Guthrie." I looked around. I had heard about the Oklahoma singer, but had never met him.

"Ask him to sing *Tom Joad*—it's a ballad he just finished. It's based on the *Grapes of Wrath*." (Everybody in New York was talking about Steinbeck's novel and the movie Hollywood had made of it.)

I walked over to the thin little man and introduced myself. We exchanged a few words, and then I asked, "About that song you've just written: would you mind singing it for us?"

"Don't mind if I do."

Woody pushed a chair into the center of the room. He put his foot on the seat, swung the guitar from his back to playing position, tuned up and strummed for a moment or two. All eyes were instantly on him. The hubbub died down quickly and everyone found a chair. The strumming began again.

> Tom Joad got out of the old McAlester Pen.
> There he got his parole.
> After four long years on a man-killing charge
> Tom Joad came a-walking down the road, poor boy,
> Tom Joad came a-walking down the road.

. . . .

> Tom Joad walked down to the neighbors farm,
> Found his family.
> They took Preacher Casey and loaded in a car
> And his mother said: "We got to git away."
> His mother said: "We got to git away."

Woody sang the long ballad from beginning to end. The silence in the room deepened, and as he sang the sad tale of the dispossessed people of the Dust Bowl, we all knew that Woody was singing the truth, telling the story of his people exactly as it happened.

We also sensed that he had the quality of greatness. Henceforth he would speak not only for the people of Oklahoma and Texas, and for the migrant workers of the peach and grape fields of California, but for all of us who lived through those troubled times.

Woody came to the station often in those days. Sometimes we turned the program over to him to sing what he liked: prison songs and British and homemade-American ballads. He loved the stories of the American bad men, of the outlaw heroes who took the law into their own hands. He sang of man-made disasters and natural disasters. But we loved most of all hearing him sing his own songs.

The man who wrote *This Land is Your Land* and *So Long, It's Been Good to Know You* was the great balladeer of the American Depression. He told the unvarnished truth exactly as he saw and experienced it in his wanderings along the highways and byways of the nation. Woody Guthrie, born in the small town of Okemah, Oklahoma, was the unofficial chronicler of his generation. The legacy he left was not an academic history, but a human document made up of a thousand songs and a large body of writings of every kind.

Woody was the poet of his people, just as Robert Burns of Scotland and Federico Garcia Lorca of Spain were of theirs. Like them and like countless epic poets and medieval minstrels, he created works that are universal and will be remembered long after the events and issues that inspired them have been forgotten. Like them, he sang the old songs of his people, revamped them to fit the times, and infused them with new life. He was an authentic American genius, a common man with uncommon gifts. In his songs and writings he combined country wit, pioneer traditions, and colorful and unhackneyed country language with a skilled writer's art. He represents, better than anyone else, the human unity of rural and urban America.

A survivor of some of America's hardest years, he transcended his personal trials without ever losing his great zest and love of life. He had more love, and more compassion for ordinary people, than anyone I have ever known.

His sense of humor was prodigious and, like every great humorist, he could stand off and laugh at himself:

> I am five feet and some inches in my brother's socks feet. My hair is wavy when I'm two haircuts behind, and plumb curly when I'm four. I ain't got any bad habits except my own, and never take a drink unless I am by myself or with somebody.

He used words with uncanny skill:

> A man's ambition is little of him, that'll always run to the boss and tell, a woman's love is often little and it's a libel that they tattle, I started to say "tittle" to rime with "little"—but switched to "tattle" to rime with "prattle," 'cause tit for tit and tat for tat, a scabbers heart beats awful flat. . . . Poet and rarin to show it.

It has been my aim in writing this book to tell the story of Woody Guthrie exactly as it happened. Some of my information has come from his published works: his autobiography, *Bound for Glory* (1943); *American Folksong* (1947); and his newspaper column, *Woody Sez* (1939–41).

Much documentation, however, came from Woody's unpublished writings, presented here for the first time. He wrote copiously about himself and fortunately kept everything. Through the generosity of Mrs. Marjorie Guthrie, I was able to consult such important works as *Boomchasers,* an earlier version of *Bound for Glory; Silver Mine,* a novel of his years in Texas; and *Stackabones,* written for the first-born child of his marriage to Marjorie.

I have also extracted data from the wealth of other material placed at my disposal by Marjorie Guthrie and the Guthrie

12

Children's Trust Fund: from Woody's numerous letters, from notes he wrote in book margins and on record albums, and from countless ruled notebooks filled in his own handwriting with commentary on his songs, his private life, and the world around him.

Woody was a man of many talents and interests, but he literally lived his music. His feelings went beyond what most people call a "love of music"; for Woody, music was a basic need, as necessary as eating, drinking, breathing. Wherever he went, his guitar went too, and he played it everywhere—in the migrant camps of California, the war-ravaged towns of Sicily, and the New York subways.

Throughout the book I have quoted Woody's own words as much as possible so that he could speak for himself—tell his story as he saw and lived it. For the same reason I have presented my interviews with Mrs. Guthrie as they happened. I saw no reason to rewrite what she had so vividly described in her own words. Many pages in the latter part of the book are given over to her reminiscences. No one knew Woody better or longer, and no one is as qualified to tell the true story of the last twenty-five years of his life.

Finally, I sifted material from the writings of others: from the recollections of Woody's friends and from the 1940 interviews with folklorist Alan Lomax at the Library of Congress. The reader will find many gaps in the narrative: lack of data on his brothers and sisters, his first wife and their three children. These lapses are not oversights but are due to the unavailability of information on these earlier years.

A generation has passed since Woody sang his first songs. We are again at war; there is poverty in the midst of plenty, and hate among our people where love should be. Again, as in Guthrie's time, society is in ferment. Again, the conscience of youth has been stirred to action, as young people become aware of the threat to the individual in the facelessness of our mechanized world.

13

In a recent letter to the Guthrie Children's Trust Fund a young admirer of Woody and his son Arlo wrote:

I am sixteen years old, and I don't really dig the older generation. All I can say is if there were more people like Woody still alive I don't think there would be anything like the "generation gap." I envy anyone who was a friend of Woody's and I really wished I'd known him. He's changed my whole idea of music and opened my eyes. Thank God our generation has Arlo. Yours truly. M.S.

So long Woody—it's been good to know you . . . .

HY NYC 1969

14

OKLAHOMA

A BOY, THE THIRD CHILD of Nora Belle Tanner and Charles Edward Guthrie, was born in Okemah, Oklahoma, on July 14, 1912. Charles, an ardent Democrat and active campaigner, named his son Woodrow Wilson Guthrie, in honor of the Presidential candidate of that year, but called him "Woody" from the very beginning.

Oklahoma had become a state only five years before, in 1907. The territory was a magnet for traders, fur trappers, and cattlemen, who were drawn by its good grassland and water and dreams of vast ranches on the endless plain. A few were adventurers and get-rich schemers, but most of the settlers were homesteaders looking for sprawling ground. The rest were Negroes and various Indian tribes.

Nora Guthrie's mother, Mary Tanner, had been one of the first log-cabin school teachers in Okfuskee County. The schoolhouse on the banks of the Deep Fork River, about fifteen miles from Okemah, was in pioneer country in those days.

The tales and songs Mary Tanner heard from the motley collection of settlers were, as her grandson recalled: "full of the wild cat, the panther, the coyote, the overgrown wolf, the mountain lion, and the fights between man and beast to settle

Okfuskee County. It was, in the quicksands and muds of the river's rising, the wind that blew and whipped from east to west in a split second, the lightning that splintered the barn loft, the snakey-railed cyclone, prairie cloudbursts, . . . fiery drouth . . . timber fires . . . in the fights of the man against all of these, that I was born and heard my mother sing to my brother Roy, and to my sister Clara."

Charles Guthrie, born in Texas cotton country, had played guitar and banjo in cowboy bands until he married Nora Tanner. But though he "hung up his deviled strings," as Woody put it, and settled down to domestic life, Charlie, as everyone called him, never gave up singing. "He was always out talking, dancing, drinking and trading with the Indians. . . . Taught me to count in Chickasaw or Choctaw, Cherokee, Sioux, Osage or Seminole dialect. He was a Clerk of the County Court and our house was full of the smells of big leather law books and poems of pomp and high dignity that he memorized and performed for us with the same wild pioneer outdoor chant as he sang his Negro and Indian square dances and Blueses."

Grandpa and Grandma Tanner built a house on their farm a few miles out of Okemah and bought Nora a piano. She learned to play the chords of the Irish and Scots songs and ballads her parents had taught her. Later on they bought one of the first phonographs in the country. "The first notes of so-called civilized music," Woody claimed, "echoed in the holler trees along Buckeye Creek and in the leaves of the sumac and the green June corn. . . ."

Coming back to town from Grandma Tanner's farm every Sunday, as he neared his house, Woody could hear his parents' voices blending in perfect harmony on hymns, spirituals and soul-saving songs. "The color of the songs," he wrote, "was the Red Man, Black Man, and the white folks."

Amazing Grace, how sweet the sound
That saved a wretch like me.

18

I once was lost but now I'm found
Was blind but now I see.

Shall I be wafted to the skies
On flower beds of ease
While others strive to win the prize
And sail through bloody seas?

At home, Nora Guthrie sang her ballads and all the children had their favorites.   Clara loved to hear the old ballad, *Under the Greenwood Siding:*

O baby, O baby, if you were mine,
All along and alone-y;
I would dress you up in scarlet so fine,
All along by the greenwood siding.

O mother, O mother, when I was yours,
You pierced me through my poor tender heart.
O mother, O mother, thou hast cut stakes,
You shall be the keeper of hell's gates.

Woody would lie on the rug listening with his chin in his hand as Nora sang *Gypsy Davy:*

It was late last night
When my lord came home
Asking for his lady. . . .

Okemah, which means "Town on A Hill" in Creek, was one-quarter Negro, one-quarter Indian, and one-half white. During the oil boom its population was to swell from 1,500 to 5,000 souls.   The land around town was nothing but brushy-sand hills with farms scattered among patches of scrub oak, sycamore, and cottonwood trees.

By the time Woody was born, Charlie Guthrie was a prosperous and important man in the community. He owned about thirty farms, raised prize cattle, bulls, and hogs. He had pedigreed bird dogs "with their family trees all printed and framed all over the house." All the children helped take care of the animals.

As a real estate dealer Charlie became active in the hurly-burly of local politics. He trained the children to help out during elections. Even before Woody could read Charlie had him out along the streets on a hay wagon singing campaign songs and making speeches . . . "and he put words in my mouth to make me poke fun at the socialists." As a young man Charlie had written two anti-socialist books, and held views that his son was never to follow.

Until Woody was two years old, the Guthries lived in a comfortable six-room house in a good section of town. It was painted bright yellow and surrounded by flowers and green lawn.

Those were the prosperous years, and Nora surrounded herself with beautiful things, but it came to a sad end one day when the beautiful house burned down. This was the first in a series of disasters which led ultimately to grinding poverty.

After the fire, Charlie bought the old London house, named after its previous owners. It was quite a comedown. The big rooms on the first floor were dug right into the side of a rocky hill, and the walls were cold and clammy.

A few nice things had been saved from the fire, but all the rest was secondhand furniture that had seen better days.

Charlie made all kinds of plans to transform the London house into a decent home for the family but they would hear none of it. They just could not reconcile themselves to living there at all.

The London house was hated by the other members of the family but Woody, as the youngest, found its good points. Best of all was the high porch along the top story, the highest in Okemah. From this lookout he could see the bottom of the hill, and watch the wagons rolling into town with entire families atop bales of cotton. He could see them driving under the shed at the gin mill, disappear and appear again with the wagons full of cotton seed. From another point he could watch the trains, hear the wild-sounding whistles and see the black smoke belching up from the smokestack. So what if London house wasn't the most beautiful place in Okemah? Woody's friends were there frequently with him, watching the trains and the cotton wagons from his porch lookout, and that was what home meant for the boy!

For no apparent reason, Nora became irrational at times, even violent, and was depressed for long periods.

She would make some excuse. "It's the London house, and it takes so much to keep it clean."

Finally she took to sitting at home by herself, never visiting anyone, never receiving visitors. Sometimes she would try to read a book but it would lie open in her lap, while her eyes stared outside.

One day, the heat was stifling. Not a breath of air stirred, not a leaf, not a blade of grass. An unexpected gust of cool air surprised Woody as he walked with his father. Dark clouds of dust were swirling along the ground, and higher, blocking out the sky. The wind swept everything in its path.

It was a great lark for Woody, but his father was alarmed. A cyclone was coming. What if its snaky black tail were to suck away the little they now had—the old London house? What would become of the family then?

As they pushed against the wind, Nora and Grandma came towards them. The rain was already pelting down. "We're heading for a shelter, here's a raincoat," they shouted, and ran for the cellar.

Charlie lifted Woody onto his shoulders, covering them both with the coat. Woody clung to his father's neck more tightly as he felt the powerful thrust of the wind and the driving rain. Tubs and planks spun around in midair. Barn doors swung loose and splintered into a thousand pieces. The storm howled and roared around them, stronger and more destructive with every passing moment.

"Keep your head down!" Charlie yelled.

Just as they came within sight of the shelter, a fresh gust of wind and rain drove them behind a cow barn. A moment later the barn was torn from the ground and lifted fifty feet in the air. The two fell forward. Charlie crawled to the cellar door dragging Woody underneath him.

"Let us in, let us in!" he yelled, banging his fists on the door. It opened a little and they squeezed through. Fifteen people huddled and shifted around the storm cellar. Several lanterns cast strange shadows on the walls. Woody climbed into his mother's lap and was sung to sleep with the words of *The Sherman Cyclone:*

> You could see the storm approaching
> And its cloud looked deathlike black
> And it was through our little city
> That it left its deadly track.

At last the door opened and a voice called in:
"The worst is over!"

As they came out, there in the distance they could see the huge black tail still whipping its way through the flat countryside. It was dreadful: groans were heard as people discovered their houses or barns smashed in. But there was also joy, as parents, children, relatives and friends hugged and kissed, grateful to find each other alive.

Roy and Clara appeared. They had been in the school cellar during the cyclone. The family climbed to the top of the hill and looked over the rim.

"There," said Charlie quietly, pointing to the house, "that's all that's left."

What had once been London house was now rubble and wreckage. The roof was gone, the rock walls almost entirely caved in. They rushed down the hill and into what remained of the house. Water and mud covered the floor. Furniture, dishes, everything was smashed, twisted, torn. Everyone burst into hysterical laughter—everyone except Charlie.

22

Finally he could stand it no longer.

"This wrecked home, this filth and slush, isn't that enough to bring you all to your senses?"

"Yes," said Nora quietly, "it has brought me to my senses. I'm glad the house is gone!"

And in fact, the demise of the London house proved to be no great loss. Okemah had moved into the prosperous twenties; there was new construction, jobs were plentiful, and Charlie began to make money again in buying and selling property. It was a good time, and the family thrived. Another son, George, was born, and while he was still an infant, Nora gave birth to Mary Jo.

In time, Charlie moved the family into a fine house on North Ninth Street on the other side of town. Woody could hear his father riding down the road a long time before he got home. The clomping of the horse's hooves rang clear on the road. When the weather was good Woody would run out to meet his father. Charlie would pull him up onto the saddle, and the two would begin a question and answer song.

Papa:	It's been a hot old, hot day.
Woody:	Yes, yes, yes, it's hot, I say.
Papa:	Where've you been, my curly head?
Woody:	I been a playin' in the big high weeds.
Papa:	Who did you play with? What did you play?
Woody:	Played bows and arrows and war all day.
Papa:	Did you have any fuss? Did you have any fights?
Woody:	One big fuss, an' two little fights.
Papa:	Woodpecker peckin' and the bark's a flyin'.
Woody:	Ole folks fussin' an' the kids a cryin'. How did y'r saddle horse do today?
Papa:	He et all my oats, an he et my hay.

They would both take the saddle, bridle, and blanket off the horse as Charlie sang:

23

My little woodhead he works like a man.

And Woody answered:

I ain't no man, but I do the best I can.

Okemah for some time had been abuzz with whispering and rumors, for tests had showed that the whole region was sitting on top of an ocean of oil. Then one day a man shot out of his flivver on Main Street and ran for the land office. "Oil," he yelled, "She's blowed her top." Within a short time, the quiet town was transformed into a wild, feverish madhouse. Thousands of people came to Okemah and filled the streets to overflowing. Oil derricks went up everywhere—along the river and creek bottoms, in pastures and on the sides of hills.

Under other circumstances the black scum might have been considered a dreadful scourge, a blight disfiguring the entire countryside. But the sight of the whirling, swirling, swelling stream of oil sliding down the river was cause for joy. Even the foul smell of oil fumes that polluted the air for miles around brought no complaints. Oil brought jokes for many, riches for a few, excitement, amusements never seen before, and people of every description.

When the sun hit it just right the black-golden oil reflected all the colors of the rainbow. It was a beautiful sight from the river or the bridge. But the fish died by the thousands, and the slender reeds and grass turned gray and never grew again. Trees and wild grape vines withered away. So much for the impact of oil on nature. About its effect on humanity, Woody later wrote:

■ Okemah became one of the singingest, square dancingest, drinkingest, yellingest, preachingest, walkingest, talkingest, laughingest, cryingest, shoutingest, fist fightingest, bleedingest, gamblingest, gun, club and razor carryingest of our ranch and farm towns.

The first people to hit town was the rig builders, cement men, carpenters, teamskinners, wild tribes of horse traders and gypsy wagons . . . crooked gamblers, pimps, whores, dope fiends, peddlers, stray musicians and street singers, preachers cussing about love and begging for tips . . . Indians . . . with their kids underfoot . . . Thousands of folks come to work, . . . celebrate, pray, sing, talk, argue and fight with the old settlers.

Thus Woody described the boom in his autobiography, *Bound for Glory*.

In other, unpublished writings, Woody turned the same sharp eye on his fellow townsmen.

■ The old settlers . . . went into business to make money off the newcomers. The newcomers worked mostly in the field, but some . . . sold burgers and bad chile, jake, liquor, bay rum, rubbing alcohol, hair tonic, extracts, to the oil field workers, sharecroppers, and town people, both Negro, Indian and white. Before the Indians got their oil money, they were allowed to marry a Negro, but not a white; and after the Indians got their money, they were allowed to marry whites, but not Negroes.

I see the boomtown from all four sides:
(1) The hometown church folks that pay the
(2) politicians and officers to clean out the
(3) dens of crooked officials
(4) and the honest, hard working people that usually hit town broke, worked to build the country up, and make the living for the . . . 3 other kinds. . . .

Fights, killings, and lynchings were commonplace, but worst of all were election days when more fights were reported than votes.

While the adults fought it out on the streets of Okemah, the kids carried on at the Gang House, a neighborhood club house built on the side of Graveyard Hill. The Gang House was the scene of Woody's earliest political education. Modeled after the local government, it had its own laws, with its own courts, judges, and sheriff to enforce them. It issued paper "money" backed up by "valuable junk," devised its own gambling schemes and land rushes. In the boom years there were fights which grew to full scale "wars" between the Boomchasers' kids and the Home Town kids over who was going to run the organization.

During the oil boom, Woody had a job selling newspapers. The toughest kids held the best selling corners and the competition was fierce. Woody knew all the landlords and they let him sell his papers inside their buildings. As a result, he got to know every gambling joint, girly place, slot machine place, cafe, and pool hall in Okemah.

He earned a few extra pennies by playing the harmonica and singing such songs as *The Sinking of the Titanic, Drunkard's Dream, Barbara Allen,* and the *Dream of the Miner's Child.*

Woody had learned to play the harmonica from a Negro shoe-shine boy who worked in the barber shop. He always played *Railroad Blues*. Woody spoke to him one day. "That is undoubtedly the lonesomest piece of music that I ever run onto in my life," he said. "Where in the world did you learn it?"

"Oh," said the boy, "I just lie here and listen to the railroad whistle. Whatever it say, I say, too."

As Woody later described it, "Every day he would play me the same piece over and over and over. He just improvised as he went along and never did play the same piece no two days alike because he is just playing something that was in his head and never wrote down."

When Charlie got on the sheriff's force, Woody hung around the jail too. He often saw the same old bootleg stills being raided and chopped full of holes by ax-wielding local church members. The stills would be displayed in the center of town for a week or so to prove that the sheriff was really cleaning up the county, and then were auctioned back to the same whiskey makers. In no time at all the stills were repaired, back in action, and operating freely until the next raid.

One dive was a combination of pool hall and poker room. Though youngsters were usually not admitted, Woody's presence was grudgingly tolerated. Each poker table had a group seated around it and about half a dozen men standing around winking and making signals to the players. Behind them another bunch watched the newcomers being fleeced by the experienced gamblers. A few would wander in and out fishing bootleg liquor out of trash cans to sell to the boys losing their money at poker.

Woody seldom sold papers in dives like that. The men were too wild, too worked up to bother with newspapers. Dice, cards, dominoes, the easy access to girls, the rotgut liquor had them "whipped up to a fever heat, jumpy, jittery, wild and reckless."

At the movie house, in steel cages, were wax dummies of Billy the Kid, Jesse James, and the "Most Famous Lady Outlaw of All Time," Belle Starr. Further down the street preachers were warning and exhorting, "The day of the coming of the Lord is near. Are you ready, brothers and sisters? Are you saved and sanctified and baptized in the spirit of the Holy Ghost? Is your soul white as the drifted snow?"

The people sauntered by. "Yes, I'm going to join the church before I die, but I wanta have some fun and live first!"

Okemah was not only the only town to strike oil, but it was one of the more stable kind. Writes Woody:

■ I rode the long coupling poles, on the wagon loads of oil field machinery, boilers, stacks, bits, stems, casing, engines, cement, horse and mule feed, and the wagons were pulled by from 2 to 20 horses or mules. I saw the new boom towns flare up and die down—Slick City, Bowlegs, Sand Springs, Springhill, Garrison City, and later Oklahoma City. I worked on an ice truck that made the shacktowns, and looked in at all the kitchens and dirty little houses, where flies from the privvy crawled over the babies' eyes ■ and mouth while they was trying to sleep.

Meanwhile, disaster hit the Guthrie family again. Clara stayed home from school one day to do the ironing and get ready for exams. She filled the old kerosene stove with coal oil and cleaned it, as she had many times before. For a while it refused to burn. She opened the stove door to look in. As the fresh air hit the chamber full of thick, greasy smoke, fire burst out and in a moment she was enveloped in flames! Screaming, she ran through the house, out into the yard and around the house several times before she finally rolled in the tall green grass to smother the fire. A neighbor's boy saw her and rushed to help extinguish the flames. It was too late. He carried her into the house and laid her poor little burned body on the bed.

Clara died the next day. She was fourteen. Nora never quite recovered from the horrible death of her daughter.

After Clara's tragedy, the family was drawn together for a while. They sought comfort in each other in their desperate need. But as time went by, it became obvious to everyone, family as well as neighbors, that Nora was growing seriously ill. She would go off into fits of depression or anguished screaming. To make things worse, Charlie was losing every cent he had and none of the old methods for scaling the ladder of success helped him one bit. He was out of favor with the local politicians and unable to make the big real estate profits of previous years.

Every day at the Guthrie home was a chapter in misery. Nora fell victim to bad spells, losing control of the muscles in her body, legs and arms. She would go into spasms, and fall on the floor. The children always knew when it began; they could see it coming over her, slowly but unmistakably. Her face would twitch into a snarl. Saliva would run down the corner of her mouth.

Nora had been one of the prettiest women in that part of Oklahoma, with dark eyes, a round, healthy face, and long black hair that glistened and gleamed from daily brushing. When she and Charlie used to ride together—she on a regal black horse fitted with a hundred-dollar side saddle, and he on a fast-paced white mare—people used to comment how pretty they looked; a little unreal, perhaps, but decorative!

Now Nora never bothered about her appearance any more and walked through town crying, utterly distraught. There were periods when she seemed to be perfectly all right but they didn't last long. The doctor finally came to the conclusion that she was hopelessly insane and urged Charlie to take her where she might be free of troubles.

Roy and Woody had to take care of the house during these years, a heavy responsibility. Roy was fifteen and Woody only nine. Every night Woody had dreams of his mother smiling and working around the house, but when he awoke, there was the house in its usual mess, the dishes piled high in the sink, and tubs of unwashed clothes in the back yard.

Every once in a while they would escape from the realities of home life and do what other boys their age did: go swimming and fishing, play hooky, and get into the gang wars. They even made home-brew liquor—in secret, for it was illegal.

■ The idea was to get one cake of yeast and let it ferment two days; but we figured it out that if we used five gallons of water along with the malt and hops and three cakes of yeast, and keep a good hot fire by it, that it would ferment in one day . . . before night it was just a-foaming and a-jumping like a whole pond full of frogs. . . . We all got sick on it and like died, the bunch of us did! I don't see
■ yet how we got to be as old as we did!

29

Charles found it difficult to adjust himself to the prospect of poverty. He still believed that he could make it again—the ten-thousand-dollar oil deals, the profits from real estate, the leases changing hands every day. But no one would help him any more, he was no longer useful to the big money of Okemah; politically, Charlie Guthrie was no longer of any account.

Unable to pay rent on the house and hoping that Nora might improve in a different place, the Guthries moved to Oklahoma City. Taking a few things with them, they drove an old Model-T truck, found an old house on Twenty-eighth Street, and set up housekeeping. There were no rugs, no furniture to speak of, no luxuries, yet Nora seemed to feel better. She began to cook again, kept the house clean, and planted sweet peas. Sometimes days would go by without Nora having a spell, and the family breathed a sigh of relief.

Hard times dogged Charlie's footsteps. He found a job selling fire extinguishers, but they didn't sell. For weeks he would tramp the streets, his clothes becoming so worn and frayed that finally he could no longer go out. A grocer gave him some foodstuff on credit and he stayed on to work around the store. This netted him a dollar a day. An old lady who had a cow paid Woody one dollar a week to deliver milk to the store. These meager earnings kept the family from starvation, though just barely: their regular diet consisted largely of beans, coffee, and fried mush.

One day when the Guthries had been in Oklahoma City about a year, a tall, good-looking, young man rode up on a flashy, black motorcycle. It was Leonard, Nora's half brother. It seemed he was running the local agency selling the new four-cylinder Ace motorcycles, and needed someone to do the office work. He offered the job to Charlie. "You'll make about two hundred dollars a month!" he promised, and rode off.

The next day was Sunday. Charlie went out for a walk and bought the Sunday paper and a package of tobacco.

When he got home he went straight to his bedroom, read the funnies, and then turned to the news.

"MOTORCYCLE ACE KILLED IN CRASH," read the headlines. "LEONARD TANNER, ACE MOTORCYCLIST, WAS KILLED INSTANTLY IN AN ACCIDENT THAT WRECKED A CAR AND A MOTORCYCLE AT A STREET INTERSECTION YESTERDAY AFTERNOON. . . . MR. TANNER WAS GOING INTO BUSINESS FOR HIMSELF FOR THE FIRST TIME. . . ."

The Guthrie family piled their few possessions into the old Model-T truck and went back home to Okemah. They headed for the east part of town, now dilapidated and teeming with mangy dogs and kids with sores on their heads. The houses were piles of junk with rotting boards and moldy floors.

The truck stopped at the Jim Cain house, named for some luckless former owner. It had never been painted and was utterly neglected. Outside, zinnias, hollyhocks, and a bit of honeysuckle climbing up the side of the house fought a losing battle with the dust.

The children inspected their new home. The bedroom and front room were crowded with tubs full of trash. All the windows were broken; the wallpaper flapped loose from the walls. Rat turds surrounded big holes in the floor boards. The smell of something dead pervaded the house.

As they unloaded the truck and carried their broken-down household goods inside, a friendly neighbor came over to help them unload the truck and install themselves in the new house.

"How long you folks been gone?"

"Exactly one year."

"Have you been down in the center of town since you got back?"

"No, we haven't."

"Well, you're in for a big surprise. This is a dead town, a ghost town. Everybody's gone."

Woody dashed out of the house, running as fast as he could,

rounded the corner at the railroad station, and stared down the entire length of Main Street. It was deadly quiet: just a few old parked cars, a few sleepy horse-drawn wagons plodding along. All the shops on the first block were nailed up. It was like a graveyard. He poked his head into the Broadway Hotel; nobody was there. Bill Bailey's old pool hall, down the street, the Yellow Dog bootleg joint, and the Monkey Oil Drug Store all were deserted. A short year before, that street had been alive with yelling, hell-raising people, the smell of good food, the sound of fiddles and yodeling, the hustlers in short skirts and overpainted faces. But now there were no crowds, no gang fights, no laughter—nothing, just a wasteland.

As he walked slowly home, discouraged and dismayed, Woody tried to think of something to say to his family, something funny. How could you joke about old dead Okemah?

To his surprise, there was his mother cheerfully humming one of her songs, handing out cups of coffee. The house was neat, the dirt and junk cleared out, chairs and sofa comfortably arranged around the room. Woody could not believe his eyes. There in the corner was Roy, smiling.

"Your father," Nora announced, "has got a new job!"

"A job? Doing what?"

"Selling automobile licenses for the state," Roy said. "He gets half a dollar for writing out papers. And I'm going to help him, and they're going to pay me too!"

For a while life was good again; Nora was in fine spirits and there was harmony and peace in the family. But only for a time.

It happened as Nora and Woody were working in the garden. Inside the house, fumigators had been lit to drive off the ever-present cockroaches. Until the air in the rooms had cleared, everyone was to stay outside. But instead of dissipating, the fumes, seeping out through cracks in the walls, gradually increased. Soon huge clouds of smoke came rolling out. Was the house on fire? Woody barely had time to worry; his eyes were fixed on his mother's face. Nora had stopped working and was staring at the house. Woody tried to talk to her, distract her, but she paid no attention to him.

Suddenly her eyes widened, her face and mouth stiffened.

As if hypnotized, Nora arose from her knees. Taking long, powerful strides, she walked toward the house. Her son raced in front of her, putting his hand out to stop her, but she swept him aside as if he were a paper doll.

Woody's heart turned to ice. He tore out of the yard, raced along a dirt road as fast as he could, his head pounding. He ran all the way to his father's office. "Run Papa, quick! It's Mama!"

In an instant, Charlie and Roy burst out of the door and ran home. They found the house in shambles, windows smashed, the kitchen charred and burned, and the bedroom in wild disarray. Nora was unharmed, but no one ever really found out what had happened inside the house.

The next day Nora was taken to the insane asylum in Norman, Oklahoma. She died there three years later, on June 30, 1930, the victim of Huntington's Disease, a rare hereditary illness that was ultimately to carry off her son Woody as well. With his mother's departure, Woody's boyhood—what was left of it—came to a sudden end.

Some time later Charlie was badly burned when an oil stove burner exploded. He spent many months in a hospital, then went to live with some wheat-farming relatives in the Texas Panhandle, where he spent eighteen months recuperating. The two younger children, George and Mary Jo, stayed with relatives in Oklahoma. The older boys were left on their own.

Roy and Woody continued to live at the Cain house for a while after their father went to Texas. With Nora gone, it had become a dirty house. The kitchen smelled sour, the garden was overgrown with weeds and dead, dry flowers. It was a ghost house; the phantoms haunted it in empty, hollow silence. When daylight filtered through the dusty windows,

33

the boys would get their clothes on and escape out into the open as soon as they could.

Roy found a job at the Okemah Wholesale House. He rented a room across town, planning to share it with his brother, but Woody decided to strike out for himself. The day they left the Jim Cain house, Woody took a quilt and blanket and moved into the old Gang House.

Woody spent every day collecting and selling junk. Each outfit he worked for baptized him in several repulsive ways: throwing him into the garbage, squirting him and covering him with every conceivable kind of rotting trash. Sometimes his sack weighed as much as fifty pounds, and he often walked ten to fifteen miles carrying it on his back. Each day he brought the sack to the city junk man to be weighed in and sold, but he always kept a few things for himself. Each night he would return to the Gang House and there he would make shapes and forms from the pieces of brass, tin, aluminum, and glass he had salvaged from his sack. This activity helped him keep his sanity.

But summer had come and the old Gang House hill smelled of rotting wood. When it rained, the water from the hill would seep into the shack. At night Woody would lie on his damp blanket, half asleep, half awake, troubled by dreams of blood and violence, slime and fire.

His dubious independence came to an end the day Roy found him lying on a bench near the school grounds, burning with fever. From that time on Woody's status changed from junk boy to free boarder with local families. At one time, he lived with a family of thirteen in a small two-room house.

"In the cold house were eleven others sleeping in two rooms. Why, us kids were big boys and girls, we had two or three beds, you know.

"So we would sleep, some of us at the head and some of us at the foot and had everybody's feet in everybody's faces."

Still, it meant a home for a few years. A later stay with a

34

more prosperous family proved to have its own problems, as he told Alan Lomax years later:

■   They had a dad-gummed little old banty hen that sat out on the icebox and roosted out there like she owned that whole part of town.   My job mainly while I was living with that family of people was to keep track of that cussed banty hen.   I had to go find the egg, where she hid the egg, what time of day she hid the egg, bring the egg in.

And then Missus Price would go out and pet the hen and then when night come I would have to go get the hen again, and set her up on the icebox to where she could be safe from all harm and I used to carry her nigh fourteen blocks across town from a livery stable in a tow sack and I would have to make a trip or two every month, by George, to get that hay for the banty hen.

So I thought, well, hell's bells, rather than be a chamber-
■   maid to a banty hen, I am going to take to the highways.

Woody's mother: Nora Belle Guthrie.

Woody's father: Charles Edward.

The young Charlie and Nora Guthrie
with Roy and Clara.

Charlie Guthrie with a
prize steer.

May 16, 1926, in Okemah, Oklahoma: Woody (left), Charlie (right), Nora (standing), George (seated).

The London House, restored in later years. Woody watched the trains from the upstairs porch.

TEXAS

IT WAS A BAD TIME to take to the highways. The country was in the grip of the disastrous Depression of 1929, and anyone traveling the roads looking for work had plenty of company. At seventeen, Woody became part of the army of migrant workers who traveled from job to job during America's worst economic slump. The ranks of the jobless were swelling to a reputed 20 million. In three years, President Franklin D. Roosevelt would be calling for a New Deal for the unemployed and depressed. In the meantime, the United States was a huge disaster area and none felt the pinch harder than the people of Texas and Oklahoma as they saw their savings wiped out by the national money crisis and their land wiped out by the dust storms.

Such was the backdrop of Woody's wanderings, as he made his way first to the Gulf Coast, then back to Okemah, and finally to Pampa, Texas, there to join his father. After recovering from his burns, Charlie Guthrie had remained in Pampa, an oil boom town in the Texas Panhandle, the big wheat belt centering around the city of Amarillo. Now he wrote to offer his son the possibility of a job. Woody left a five-dollar-a-week stint in a filling station and hit the road again. He was

{ to make Texas his home until 1937, working on the fringe of the oil industry, raising a family, and writing his first songs.}

Woody always claimed that the Pampa-Amarillo area "where the wheat grows, the oil flows, and the farmer owes" was also where the blackest and thickest storms blew. There one could see dust storms of every "color, flavor, description, fashion, shade, design, and model." The wide, flat prairies of the Panhandle had once looked like an endless sea of wheat; now there was a sea of dust, rippling in the wind, smothering the land beneath it.

"We watched the dust storm come up," said Woody, "like the Red Sea closing in on the Israel children." The sight was so frightening that people congregated in different houses around town, seeking solace in each other's company. Men, women, and children would crowd together, hardly able to see each other's faces in the sudden darkness. Strong electric light bulbs, hanging in the middle of a room, seemed to give off about as much light as a glowing cigarette end.

The sun was blotted out at noon and religious people didn't have to go far for analogies:

"Well, boys, girls, friends and relatives, this is the end. This is the end of the world. People ain't been living right. The human race ain't been treating each other right. They have been robbin' each other and shooting around. And the fellow that made this world, He sent us this dust storm."

Now it was time to go, time to cross the river to Death and time to say goodbye to each other.

"Well, so long, it's been good to know you."

It was a Pampa storm that inspired one of Woody's most famous songs. This particular dust storm—one of the worst ever to hit Texas—blew into Pampa on April 14, 1935. It seemed the omen of Doom and it led Woody to sum up the despair of those times.

So long, it's been good to know you
So long, it's been good to know you

So long, it's been good to know you
This dusty old dust is a-gettin' my home,
I've got to be driftin' along.

I've sung this song but I'll sing it again
Of the place that I lived on the wild, windy plains
In the month called April, the County called Gray
And here's what all of the people there say:
So long, etc.

The telephone rang and it jumped off the wall
That was the preacher a-making his call
He said "Kind friend, this may be the end,
And I've got a cut price on salvation of sin."

The churches was jammed, the churches was packed,
That dusty old dusty storm blowed so black
The preacher could not read a word of his text,
He folded his specs and he took up collection, said:
So long, it's been good to know you, etc. . . .

Pampa in the Depression was hardly more than a scattering
of little run-down shacks built of rotten lumber, box crates,
and flattened oil barrels.   They were temporary shelters, since
most of the workers stayed only long enough to install the machinery and insure the steady flow of oil.   By the time Woody
moved to Pampa the main part of the boom had gone.   Every
once in a while a new gusher would open and the town would
revive for a time.   Once the oil wells were in—the holes
drilled down fifteen thousand feet, the valves capping the high
pressure gushers, and the oil flowing steadily—there was little
for the oil workers to do.   They would move out of town as
broke and down and out as the first day they came into the
camp.
    The laborers who came to the oil fields were mostly country
people.   There was no more work to do on the farm, so they

came looking for the high wages and the many jobs they had heard about. They were proud people, hard workers, no matter how exhausting the toil. And they rode hundreds of miles down the highway to the oil camps.

Charlie Guthrie had a job managing a row of buildings, a honeycomb of dives and dens, rickety fire traps. Woody was the handyman. He cleaned rooms, collected the rents, was chambermaid and "broom waltzer," learned all the goings-on, how the workers got worked, and the crooks got outsmarted. "The whiskey line, the dope ring, flop joints, the hardest workers in the field, best fighters, and the cheapest laundries—I saw the whole works," he wrote later on.

In the rooming houses throughout the boom town area, the walls were so thin you could hear everything from a whisper to a shout, the creak of a bedspring, the thump of a chair being moved from one part of a room to the other. The oil workers called the rhythm of the bedspring creak "the rusty spring blues." Woody claimed that after a minute of listening he could guess the weight of the roomer to within three pounds.

The girls that came to the boom towns lived in rooming houses such as Charlie Guthrie managed. Many of them were church-going country girls with work-reddened hands. They learned very quickly to adapt themselves to new ways, spending their first wages on nail polish, high-heeled shoes, cigarettes, and corn liquor. Shy at first, they soon learned to imitate the slang, the small talk of the old-timers. Some of them got jobs in cafes and hotels but there was never enough work of that kind to go around.

The women did their best to make the shacks livable but they fought a losing battle. No matter how they tried mopping, scrubbing, and cleaning, the floors remained crooked, the linoleum worn. And nothing could stop the dust. It seeped through the cracks, piled up in drifts on the floor, settled in people's hair, and streaked their faces black. Everyone breathed the dust into his lungs, and many came down with what was called "dust pneumonia." In *Dust Pneumony*

44

Blues, Woody was to describe the condition with a certain gritty humor:

I've got that dust pneumony, pneumony in my lung,
I've got that dust pneumony, pneumony in my lung,
And I'm gonna sing this dust pneumony song.

I went to the doctor, and the doctor said, my son,
Yes, I went to the doctor, and the doctor said, my son
You got that dust pneumony and you ain't got long, not
    long.

Now there ought to be some yodelling in this song,
There ought to be some yodelling in this song,
But I can't yodel for the rattling in my lung.

Down in Texas my gal fainted in the rain,
Down in Texas my gal fainted in the rain,
I throwed a bucket o' dirt in her face just to bring her
    back again.

Once, tired of waltzing the broom at the boarding house, Woody got a job working a "root beer" stand. It paid a handsome three dollars a day.

"Now in addition to this root beer," the owner told Woody, "here's some bottles of another description." And he reached under the counter. "If anybody comes up and lays a dollar and a half on the counter, why you reach down and gently and firmly let him have one of these here bottles."

One day Woody's curiosity got the best of him. He opened a bottle and tasted whatever it was that cost half a day's salary. One fiery swallow told the whole story: it was pure unadulterated corn whiskey—a profitable item in those days of Prohibition.

The whiskey store, however, played a role in Woody's musical education. The owner kept a guitar there and when there were no customers Woody spent his time picking out tunes and experimenting with chords.

Woody really learned how to play the guitar from his father's half brother, Jeff, a local deputy sheriff and one of the best fiddlers in the Texas Panhandle. Jeff called his two fiddles the "squawling panther" and the "wild cat in a Lost Canyon." An apt pupil, Woody was soon picking up extra money, accompanying his uncle at ranch and farmhouse dances, at Chamber of Commerce banquets, and at rodeos and "bust-down parties."

For some time, Jeff had been buying magic tricks through the mail and practicing at home. It was positively dangerous to walk around, for everything had a way of disappearing and reappearing. Strings and wires were fixed in such a way that you stumbled over yards of it every time you visited the house.

At last, in a burst of ill-advised enthusiasm, Jeff left the police force, and with $500 he had saved went into the magic-show business. Woody decided to go along. He quit his job at the whiskey store, bought an old gray wig, some chin whiskers and spirit gum, and joined his uncle's small company of players.

Jeff's wife Allene came along as accordionist and chief assistant. Her name was printed right across the accordion and set off with fake diamonds guaranteed to shine like the crown jewels.

Woody played the part of a bumbling comedian, stumbling over the trigger strings and wires, exploding guns, and setting skeletons dancing, rabbits hopping, and chickens flying.

Sometimes things went wrong. Then Woody would have to hold the attention of the crowd by telling stories, playing his harmonica, and singing while Jeff got the flying springs and balony sausages working right under his tuxedo jacket. When it was over, the folks shook hands and invited them back. But the money that came in rarely paid for their food; nor did it quite cover the cost of gas and oil for the car.

For a brief time, the magic show traveled on a shoestring to every town and village in the Panhandle; then it folded. Who, in that miserable winter of 1931–1932 had money for groceries, let alone the price of a ticket to a magic show? One wintry night they played their last performance in the town of Old Mobeetie, just across the Oklahoma line. Their money was gone and Pampa was far away. If they tried, they might reach Jericho, Texas, where Allene's family, the Boydstuns, lived. Jeff headed the car toward Jericho.

It was a cold, snowy, sloshy night. The chains rumbled under the fenders. The mud and the sticky Texas gumbo soil clogged the wheels. It was a frightful trip. Now and then the car would stop, and everyone would pile out into the freezing night to pry or kick off the mud that glued itself stubbornly to the tires.

As things turned out, they weren't the only ones to make their way to Jericho. By mid-winter, Maud and Robert Boydstun's house had become the refuge for down-and-out friends and relatives—including Charlie Guthrie, who had lost his job in Pampa. Cliff and Lesley, two cowboy guitar-pickers who had appeared in some of the magic shows, dropped in for food and shelter. With Allene, Jeff, and Woody the grand total came to eight hungry, shivering adults.

Once the Boydstuns' small store of food disappeared into eight stomachs, the household fell back on sugar syrup and cornbread as a steady diet. Sometimes they roasted corn meal for coffee. When things really got bad, Robert Boydstun would walk two miles to a neighbor's house, begging for a handful of flour.

The Boydstuns were farming people. Robert, whose father and mother had been homesteaders in the Amarillo wheat country when Indians roamed the Texas plains, had planted 640 acres a year for more than 40 years. Robert could remember standing belly deep in the threshed wheat, scooping it into the bins with a big shiny steel shovel, loading it on the truck, hauling it over rough country roads to the elevator, and then heaving it onto freight cars. He had worked hard and never asked any questions.

Now here it was, the middle of the winter, and neither he nor Maude knew where their next biscuit was coming from. They had raised enough wheat in their time to feed ten generations but the land was no longer their own. High winds and hundreds of dust storms made farming precarious, but they had somehow survived the weather. The trouble in their lives began when gas-engined combine harvesters took over and did with two men what forty used to do. The competition was too great. The bank sent the sheriff to foreclose on the property. Penniless, with no one to turn to, they moved into an old ramshackle, draughty house, with little furniture, no tools, and a bare cupboard. Robert's pride was hurt; he was a man, not a dog to be kicked out into the cold.

They lived through the month-long blizzard as best they could. Charlie and Robert played dominoes day and night, huddling in front of the little stove for warmth.

When Charlie tired of dominoes, he wrote long love letters to a lady, a trained nurse he had met through the mails. Each day he sent her two pages covered with carefully written script even though the pain in his twisted fingers made the going rough.

The house was kept fairly lively with music. Jeff played the fiddle, Cliff the guitar, and Lesley sang. Woody thumped on the guitar, and learned old-time songs from the old folks. With Allene wheezing away on her accordion, the band sounded pretty good. When the spirit (or the freezing temperature) moved them, they danced as Woody sang his own song:

> Grab your partner, swing around
> Kiss yo' honey and go to town!
> Hug yo' gal like swinging on a gate
> Meet yo' partner and promenade.

Hurry up, boys and don't go slow
It may be the last time, I don't know.

Cliff made a guitar for Lesley out of a white oak wagon, and the two sang cowboy songs all the time. One of their favorites was *Chisholm Trail*, a plain talking song:

I went to the boss to draw my roll
He figured me out nine dollars in the hole.
Refrain
Come—a ki-yi-yippy-yippy yea, yippy yea
Ki-yi-yippy-yippy yay.

Sell my outfit quick as I can
I won't punch cattle for no dam man.

I'm going downtown to draw my money
Going downtown to see my honey.

With my knees in the saddle, my feet to the sky
Kiss my Hoss and say good-bye.

There was always plenty of talk. Charlie loved to sound off on politics and the law, and never let anyone forget that as a young man he had been a ripsnorting, fast-thinking, dynamic Democrat. Even though he had been almost cremated alive and his belly and chest were scarred with mismatched, overlapped skin, he was still a hard-fighting man with plenty of spunk left in him. When it came to politics Charlie's word counted the most.

Robert, a giant of a man, was a Bible expert. He could quote scripture like a preacher and believed with all his might that the Bible would tell him what was wrong with the world and how to put it right. He never found the answer, but he kept looking and looking for years.

When the worst of the winter was over, Woody went back into "show business," this time for a wheat-farm auctioneer. His new boss had just married a mail-order wife who had been a Kansas City chorus girl since 1908. (There was no doubt about the date—it was tagged on all of her costumes.) The show was a come-on to bring crowds to local auctions.

They got a job selling off a farm at Brownwood, Texas, and set up shop on a pecan bayou. The auctioneer, never one to spend his money recklessly, "drove 90 miles to save 30¢ on a box of long bolts." He pitched the tent a quarter of a mile from the highway, and put up a ten-cent light bulb at the front door.

The chorus-girl wife did her dance to the fiddle band, and it went over all right, but there was practically no one in the audience. They put on a show called "The One and Only Original Life Story of the Famous Outlaw Jesse James," starring a fly-by-night actor and the chorus girl. Next morning she was gone. So was the actor. The boss did his best to auction off the farm, but it was no use without the chorus girl. The next day he hauled the company back to Pampa, several hundred miles away.

Woody's only pay on that occasion was the boss's old typewriter. Later he wrote several plays and books on it, "but none of it," he said, "was produced in any large quantity, if any." Money would have been handier, because Woody was getting married.

Mary Jennings was the sister of a string musician who played in a local band along with Woody. The Jennings were no further up the social ladder than the Guthries, so the bride and groom set up housekeeping in a broken-down hut at the edge of town. Woody went to work in a drug store and when that job folded, took up painting store signs for Thanksgiving, Christmas, rodeos, and firemen's and policemen's balls. But as hard as he worked, he never seemed to make enough money to pay for food, rent, clothing. It was 1933, a rock-bottom year, even for the Depression.

[Much is still unknown about this first marriage. Few records were kept in those unsettled times and Woody's own writings are of little help in this case. We do know that Mary bore Woody three children: the girls, Teeny and Sue, were born in Pampa, and Bill Guthrie was born later in California. Mary's life with Woody was difficult from beginning to end, plagued by dire poverty, the hardships of traveling cross-country with the children, and frequent separations.]

· The Guthrie men were travelers, spurred on by the uncertainty of where the next dollar was coming from. Years after he had left Texas, Woody wrote a long story about the family's search, in the early 30's, for a lost silver mine once located and claimed by Grandfather Guthrie.

Like so many other accounts of his travels, *Silver Mine* mentions nothing of Mary, although it seems likely that they were already married at the time. If so, Mary probably stayed with her family in Pampa for the duration of this trip, as she would for the duration of so many more. Families frequently helped each other out in this way, but it set a pattern of living that Mary found increasingly hard to accept once she had children to care for.

How much of *Silver Mine* was based on fact, and how much was fiction, may never be known, but the story presents in graphic terms the atmosphere of desperation and frustration of those terrible years. A short version follows:

When life was good in the oil fields nobody bothered speculating on the Guthrie mine but now, in hard times, it was an absorbing topic, even though everyone had heard the story a dozen times. Uncle Jeff would lead off:

"My dad, Jerry P. Guthrie, found a mine in 1902. He had spent thirty-five years riding horseback, herding cattle, and prospecting for gold and silver, and he really knew the Mexican border country near the Chisos Mountains. One day he was out with two of my brothers. While he was having a drink from a mineral stream they knocked off a piece of rock." That chunk, the story went on, contained sixty dollars in silver and four in gold. Presumably the rest was still there, waiting.

It was a harebrained scheme, but the Guthries had nothing to lose. (The family now included Roy, come over from Okemah.) One day Jeff, Charlie, Roy and Woody headed out from Pampa to search for Grandpa Guthrie's lost silver mine. Their first destination was Sam Nail's ranch near the Chisos Mountains where the mine was supposedly located and where they hoped to get directions from the rancher. Jeff had bought a rickety truck for twenty dollars and also nine dollars' worth of supplies: two beatup guns, a handful of bullets, a fifty-five-gallon-drum of gasoline, and some food for the trip. They also took Jeff's fiddle and Woody's guitar. Then they drove six hundred miles, from Pampa to the desert near the Mexican border, and towards the Chisos Mountains looming in the distance.

The dawn made everything a purple-gray color. It was still too dark to see the narrow one-lane road (the headlights hadn't worked for a long time), so Woody sat on the front fender shining a flashlight straight ahead. "The morning floated, swayed, creaked, and buckled in the cool canyons of cold air and then darted like deers over the steep, rocky trails that took you to the top of the mountains and into the sun."

They had been climbing for some time. Soon a small washed-out-looking adobe hut came into view. "There, that's Sam Nail's place," Jeff shouted over the noise of the engine. They drove gingerly around the canyon, two more miles of twisting, then through a long, swinging cattle gate, and finally stopped in front of a house half hidden under tall cottonwood trees and mesquite.

Woody knocked on the door and knocked again, but nobody answered. He started to knock once more.

"Good morning, strangers," said a man right behind them. A handsomely dressed man in rancher's clothes stood before them. "I'm Sam Nail. What can I do for you?"

Woody explained the object of their visit. "First thing we

have to locate," said Woody, "is a place called Slick Rock Gap."

"Slick Rock Gap," Sam thought for a minute. "There's one hell of a slick wall cut through those mountains, Christmas Mountains, we call them." He pointed north.

"Next we have to find a spring which old Jerry called Toilet Springs."

"Story goes," continued Woody, "You'd take one drink of that medicine water and make a run for the nearest bush. How many of these laxative springs around here?"

Sam laughed and shook his head. "There is only one. The trouble is that it changes its location all the time. You'll know where they had been by the white formation on the rocks.

"That's going to set us back," said Woody, beginning to worry.

The truck rolled down the hill to the old adobe house they had passed on their way in, which Sam told them they could use while they were on the hunt.

Uneasy because of what Sam Nail had told them, Jeff and Woody left immediately to start the search while the others stayed behind.

As they jumped from rock to rock and scaled cliffs, loose rocks gave way beneath them, smashing into little pieces as they hit the canyon floor. They came upon white deposits everywhere, but no springs, not a trickle of water anywhere. At one point Jeff took off his shoe to scrape off the sticky mud that had stuck to it, and inadvertently dropped it. It fell straight down, irretrievably down, to the floor of the desert—miles below, it seemed. Discouraged, Jeff and Woody made their way painfully back to the old adobe house, sharp cactus needles piercing their shoes as they walked.

The first day's search had been a total failure.

That evening, in glum silence, they ate their meal of pork and beans and fried corn meal mush. The light from the one lantern in the shack illuminated every face. Jeff was doing some hard thinking. Roy sat in front of the fire occasionally spitting at the coals; Charlie occupied himself with washing the dirty dishes. It was a lonesome place.

Suddenly there was a knock at the door. Jeff opened it to see two tough-looking men with thick whiskers standing outside on the porch.

"Come in," said Jeff, looking them over. "You fellers want anything?"

"We're looking for wetbacks," said one of the strangers.

"Mister," said Woody, "there ain't no wetbacks in this house! Hell, I ain't had a bath in two weeks!"

The cops ignored him.

"Where did you get them guitars?" the first one asked suspiciously, pointing to the instruments. "Them's Mexican, ain't they?"

"Listen," said Jeff, "we don't know what you're talking about. There's nobody here but us."

"Who belongs to them Mexican guitars there?" He nodded his head again in the direction of the instruments.

"Fiddle's Jeff's. The guitar's mine," said Woody.

"Let's see you take those ukes and play us a tune! If you can't play, I'll know a wetback Mexican is hiding out there in the cactus."

Jeff and Woody picked up the fiddle and guitar and started to play. Jeff hunched his head down between his shoulders, closed his eyes, and bit his tongue. That was the way he fiddled when he was mad. His right hand moved back and forth like a fast triphammer. His playing grew louder and louder, while Woody followed him on the guitar as best he could and sang at the top of his lungs:

> Old Judge Parker!
> Take my shackles offa me!
> Old Judge Parker!
> Take the shackles offa me!

You'd better turn my
People free!
You'd better turn my
People free!

Shacklin' chain's
A-holdin' me!
Shacklin' chain's
A-holdin' me!

The first cop jumped up and danced around on his toes, then grabbed Roy and stomped around the room. All of a sudden the second officer threw back his head and howled like a wild coyote: "Yoowww!" Then he danced into the dark part of the room, hooting like some crazy bird.

When the music stopped, the first cop said, "Best damn fiddling I ever heard! Sorry we troubled you, but we gotta go!"

The two men walked away in the dark.

After the officers had gone, the Guthries quieted down, dog-tired by now. They slept on the floor, using quilts and bed-rolls. The night was bitter cold and everyone burrowed into the covers as deeply as he could.

Suddenly Roy sat up. "What's that?"

They all listened. Something was moving about. They could hear snorting and grunting and feet hitting the ground just outside the windows. The puffing and breathing got louder, and closer.

"Keep the lantern lit," Charlie told Jeff. "Woody, hand me that gun!" Jeff aimed his pistol down at the boards where the sniffing was coming from.

"Wait," whispered Charlie, "don't shoot. You can't see him and you might only wound him. And he'd tear this whole house plumb down and everything in it to boot."

"God amighty!" said Jeff, looking out at the south window. "Two cats! And ten feet high!"

Sure enough, two mountain lions faced each other outside

the hut. Pretty soon the two animals met. The growling and groaning turned into evil-sounding snarls. Then there was a screech and a rip, and a big thump hit the ground. The whines and growls continued outside. The two lions rolled on the gravel, cutting each other's bellies with their claws.

Jeff could stand it no longer. With one leap he dove out through the window, gun in hand. He shot into the brush as the first lion escaped, then shot across a clearing after the second one.

Slowly, Jeff walked back. There in front of the house was the half-eaten, bloody carcass of the goat the two lions had fought over.

Once inside, Jeff leaned against the wall, tears in his eyes, his body shaking all over. "I'm leaving this blood-sucking, lowdown desert right now. Home, that's where I'm going. I was a damn fool for coming here in the first place."

"Count me out, I'm not going with you," said Woody. "Just give me a ride to the main highway. I'm heading for El Paso."

"What for?"

"To see W. W. Turney. He was with Grandpa Guthrie when he found the mine, and he has the assay papers."

"But that was thirty-five years ago, Woody," said Charlie. "If you bring Turney in on the deal, he'll want half of the damn mine just for lending you a few dollars.

"Just because Turney is a blood relative," he continued, "that don't mean anything. He don't go by no kinfolks. He runs a money bank, not a blood bank!"

"I still got to go to EL Paso." Woody paced the floor. "But I'll promise you one thing: I won't sign no paper."

Guitar, fiddle, boxes, blankets, quilts, lantern, and rolls of clothes were loaded onto the truck. A cloud of blue smoke puffed up around the truck as it sidled out onto the road, with Jeff at the wheel, Roy in the cab with him, Charlie and Woody in the back standing up. The truck jerked along the

56

road, tired and as worn out as its passengers.   It was pitch dark and freezing, "colder than an icebox full of home brew."

Roy and Woody crawled out on the fenders, illuminating both sides of the road with their flashlight and lantern.   Fumes from the engine burned their eyes.   Soon the flashlight began giving out.   The road wound its way upward, invisible in the dark night, Roy and Woody jumping out now and then to haul the wheels of the truck around the worst of the curves.   The truck now rolled down a hill, Roy standing on the running board twisting the steering wheel with one hand.

On they went, around a steep curve, and up another thousand feet, and down three more miles.   The sound of the motor was almost drowned out by the whistling of high pressure steam when they hit the mountain top.   Now the road took them straight down to the bottom.

"Cliff banks blurred past my eyes," wrote Woody, "like the gray and brown walls of a circus tent in the dark.   Rocks and their shadows twisted and curled into a million screwy shapes in the road and wiggled off to the sides.   Bushes and trees jumped up like giraffes and long strings of elephants with their rear ends dancing out along the road.   Weeds with no shape at all turned into wild turkeys and fluttered their wings running through the sands."

The radiator boiled on Woody's right side.   The wind froze his left side.   The hot scorched oil smoke blew into his face.   He bounced around, and it felt as if his guts were sloshing up and down "like loose kidney on a meat wagon."   He jolted off his seat on the fender and slid down into the V-shaped space between the fender and the motor.

The next thing he knew the sun was shining into his eyes.   "Woodrow!   Wake up, take a taste of this.   Wake up!"   Jeff, Charlie, and Roy were bending over him.   The truck had stopped and he was lying on a mattress with a pillow under his head.   Everything was warm and the air smelled clean and fresh.

"Talk to us, Woody boy."   It was his father's voice.

"I'm fine, just dead for sleep," said Woody, reviving.

He looked up and down the street.

"What town is this?"

"Marathon.   Right on the main highway."

It was a little cowtown, with rotten saloons, half-collapsed adobe huts, and Mexican cowboys with their hats cocked against the sun.   The place smelled strongly of horse manure.

"Well, I'm leaving you here.   See you some time!   I'll write.   I'm going to take good care of myself."

He slid down from the truck with his guitar slung over his back, steered himself over to one side of the highway and waved his hands in the air.

Charlie stood up in the truck with a smile on his face and tried to wave his hand on the high wind.   Then he rubbed his hands across his eyes and slumped down on the mattress.

Woody stood in the middle of the highway, watching the old Model T disappear in the distance.   Part of him, he felt, was still on that old wreck of a truck.

Mrs. Turney, Charlie's great aunt, had written that she would be happy to see any of the Guthrie family if they ever came through El Paso.   When Woody arrived he looked in the telephone directory and found the address.   His feet hot and blistered, his clothes damp with perspiration from the long, miserable trip, he walked all the way across town.

There on a hill stood a huge mansion with big marble columns occupying a solid block.   Rose bushes, carefully tended hedges, and palm trees were planted everywhere.

Woody rang the bell.   A man opened the door.

"Whom do you wish to see, sir?"

"I'm a stranger here," he said.   "I just wanted to know if this is the City Hall?"

"I'm sorry, this is not City Hall.   You'll find it down in the central part of town."

"I made a mistake.   Sorry I bothered you."   Such houses were not part of Woody's world.   He hurried all the way down the hill.

58

He picked up a little cash singing in a bar, and then rode back to Pampa in an open cattle car on the railroad. Years later he wrote of that trip:

■   Twenty-five of us rode one night down on the Mexican Border, whistling out of El Paso, Texas, over the mountains, across the flats, and down across the mesas, and the wind was as cold as ice, and the train was making 50. Well sir, we dern near froze. We got so cold we had to get up and walk and trot back and forth in the manure on the floor to keep from freezing stiff as a Fifth Ave. face. So we run till we give out, and had to rest. Then we got stiff again. If we started a fire in the cattle car, they'd throw us in jail. So we all commenced to huddle around like a herd of sheep. Like this, you would set down, and some body would set down in your lap, and some body in his lap, and some body in his lap till we formed a big ring, every body setting in every body's lap. You didn't know who's. You couldn't see who's. You dam sure didn't care who's. You was just a grappling there in the dark—but there's a warm heat about a live human being that you are mighty thankful for when you've been out in the cold so
■ long.

Woody arrived home so frozen, it took several days in bed to thaw him out.

In the spring Charlie Guthrie came back to Pampa too. The mail-order nurse he had corresponded with arrived on the train one fine day and rushed into his arms. They rode in a taxi to the office of the Justice of the Peace and were duly married.

Betty Jean was a friendly, attractive woman of strong build. The family asked no questions about her past and she didn't bother to enlighten them. At the same time, however, she reunited the family. George and Mary Jo, Woody's younger brother and sister, had been boarding with other relatives since their mother's final illness. Betty Jean sent for the youngsters and welcomed them with open arms. She really liked having children around her.

When Betty Jean couldn't find work as a nurse, she earned a living selling mail-order clothes in the various oil camps. Even Charlie got a job for a short time as deputy to the constable.

She wasn't much of a cook and not given to housework. Still, she firmly believed that everyone should have a job to do, so Mary Jo and George kept the household going, doing the chores and preparing the meals after school. The system was a success; the Guthries enjoyed peace and comfort for the first time in many years.

The new Mrs. Guthrie was nothing if not resourceful. Hard times had come to the oil fields, the workers were leaving in droves, and Betty Jean's mail-order business collapsed. One day she put an ad in the local paper and started reading palms and telling fortunes. She used every method from psychic mind reading to "The Great White Brotherhood of Senders and Receivers of the Life Principle," as Woody called it.

No one, not the Chamber of Commerce, the banker or the preacher, knew the answer to the bank foreclosures, the dust storms, and unemployment, so everyone came as a last resort to the fortune teller's door.

Betty Jean tried to convince the children that she had some special power within her that could influence others. She must have convinced a great many grownups too, because the money started rolling in. Roy made the appointments, and there were days when more than a hundred people came to see her. On really lucrative days she would lavish crazy sums of money on the children. Charlie, out of work again, was beside himself, but there was nothing he could do. It was her money that kept the family alive.

For Woody it was a time of soul searching. He was past twenty, with a young wife and children and no visible means

60

of support. Even the menial jobs never lasted. It galled him to accept Betty Jean's handouts, but he had to think of his small family. As he walked the streets, he wondered where he was going and why there always seemed to be more people than jobs. His whole life was one big question mark, but he had never fooled himself into thinking that anyone but he himself could provide the answer. Every night he carried armfuls of books home from the local library, looking for something that might turn him into the kind of human being he wanted to be—free to work for himself, yet free to work for everybody.

He read everything he could find: political philosophy, the arts, medicine, and the law. To him, the law was too tiresome; one had to memorize so much; social theories, the sciences, led nowhere. Then he wanted to be a doctor. With the help of an old doctor's microscope, Woody investigated the murky life of microbes. He would spend hours peering down the black tube, tracking down amoebas and other invisible creatures as they whirled into life, ate their weaker brethren, or were eaten by others.

Woody also began to paint. He spent every cent he could on tubes of oil paint, canvas, and fine sable brushes. This interest in the graphic and plastic arts was one that had begun years before. As a boy left on his own in Okemah, his mother in the hospital and his father badly burned, he had earned his living gathering and selling junk. Most of it he sold for cash but he kept bits of glass, wood, machinery, and china for himself. From these he would make collages, bas-reliefs, and sculpture. His ability to create beauty out of nothing, and his interest in the arts, remained with him the rest of his life.

Woody worked hard, making copies of famous canvases, and painting dozens of heads of Christ, together with the "cops who killed him." To earn a living he went back to painting cheap signs, and adding pictures, for store windows, hotels, blacksmith shops, and funeral parlors. But the meager earnings were hardly enough to cover the cost of materials, much less support Mary and the girls.

Eventually, he wound up in the "Nothing To Nothing Mental Business," as he called Betty Jean's palm, card, and fake mind reading. Hundreds of people got his name mixed up with hers and came to his shack by mistake. To help those who needed advice, he hung a sign out telling them to come in and talk it over.

The people who knocked on his door came with a strange assortment of maladies and problems. Woody played the role of healer, prophet, financial adviser and seer: where was the best place to buy an oil field, when to buy and sell livestock, how to cure head sores, how to cure speechlessness, how to use painting as therapy for the insane. But in the end he tired of the "mind business" and went back to music, which he loved even more than painting. "A picture you buy once," he used to say, "but you can sing a song and then sing it again."

Woody began writing songs during his years in Texas. How many he actually wrote we shall probably never know, but among his vast legacy of published and unpublished works is a collection of fourteen signed songs which bear the dateline 1935. Two others with no date are attributed to one Alonzo M. Zilch, a pseudonym he used in 1941. In true minstrel tradition, Woody set his words to popular tunes, explaining the reason why in an introduction entitled *Author's Apology:*

- At times I cannot decide on a tune to use with my words for a song. Woe is me! I am then forced to use some good old, family-style tune that hath already gained a
- reputation as being liked by the people.

Continuing in this bogus antique style, he writes:

- As you turn into the pages of this book, I hope you will not have classical music on your mind . . . for there is nothing within these pages that tends to stimulate one's

mind classically.   I do not claim to be classical.   I do not
claim to be educated musically—nor to be an expert at my
■ trade. . . .

The last words trail off on the page.   The songs are in
classic American style: robust, salty, sentimental, and
humorous.   Woody sang a number of them over a bootleg
radio station his friends operated that year.   Here and there
is a hint of the socially aware Guthrie of the later Dust Bowl
Ballads, but most of the songs deal with the familiar charac-
ters and situations of old-time American folksongs.

In *Cain't Do What I Want To,* Woody observes the younger
generation:

> This younger generation
> Is the worst I've ever seen;
> Imitation eyebrows—
> And dancing jellybeans;
> They ride in automobiles,
> And flirt beneath the trees;
> I cain't do what I want to do
> But I kin think just what I please.
>
> The old saloon and picture show,
> The stylish boys and girls,
> They ain't like me and paw wuz;
> They're living in a different world.
> Don't do no good to beg them;
> Don't do no good to preach;
> I cain't do what I want to do,
> But I can think just what I please.

In 1941 when Woody was looking over these songs, he wrote at
the bottom of the page, "I figured this was hot stuff when I
wrote it. . . . But I don't know how I feel now.   I was trying
to say something—didn't know what."

That well-worn cowboy idyll, *Home On The Range,* has

been punctured in countless parodies. Woody did a new hatchet job:

> O, leave me alone
> Said his darling, his own,
> I'm not in the humor to play;
> He was amazed when he heard
> Her discouraging words—
> He decided he'd better not stay.
>
> *Chorus*
> Strange, strange, it is strange!
> She was getting more stubborn each day;
> All that he heard was discouraging words,
> And her love, it was fading each day.

If I Was Everything on Earth offered Woody's personal solution for the ills of the Depression:

> If I was President Roosevelt,
> I'd make the groceries free—
> I'd give away new Stetson hats,
> And let the whiskey be.
> I'd pass out suits of clothing
> At least three times a week—
> And shoot the first big oil man
> That killed the fishing creek.
> . . . .
>
> Woody Guthrie
> (5/35)

One of the best ballads in the collection is called *Maggie Mozella McGee,*

> The light of the limehouse
> Was burning so dim

64

Mine eyes they could scarcely see
A figure so stark standing
There in the dark
'Twas Maggie Mozella McGee.

And she had a lover
Both stalwart and brave
Who courted the ladies quite free,
And a favorite lassie
He often did see
Was Ellen Estrella De Lei.

And Ellen Estrella
Came soon into view.
Quite active and robust was she,
The same to a hair
In size when compared
To Maggie Mozella McGee.

Mozella stepped out;
In the midnight did shout:
You've taken my lover from me!
Prepare then to fight
For your love and your life,
Miss Ellen Estrella De Lei.

.   .   .   .

Ten thousand years later
A soul will not know
Who won the fray on the bay;
One had received her
A watery grave—
And the other had stolen away.

But each night at midnight,
A rumble is heard—
And the sound it doth quake like the sea,

And a ghastly white form
Disappears in the storm,
Now, is it McGee, or De Lei?

(5/5/35)

Woody's parodies were those of a man who needed to laugh, but a poet was developing beneath the broad humor. In a letter greeting a newborn niece, Woody gave eloquent expression to his developing credo, a mixture of religious belief and faith in his fellow man:

May your days be toward a glittering harvest when your seasons blend at noontide and your morning stoops to kiss your midday.

May your gladness ripen as a yellow sweetfruit and the radiance of your thinking invigorate the world.

May you forget yourself in serving others as the raindrops dash themselves to pieces to cool the dusty earth.

May you see the non-reality of affliction and realize the allness of God.   For God is truth, love.

May you never include the word enemy in your vocabulary.

May you express your innermost self nobly.

May you glance into various world religions and philosophies and form a conception of true worth and value as a highest standard of worthy purpose.

May you pass beyond the seventh veil and solve the riddle of human life and destiny.

May your good deeds lead you to the highest physical, mental, development and mastery possible.

May you attain.

With Love Always,

W. Guthrie—
.The soul doctor.

Okemah High School freshman class, 1926–27:
Woody is in the front row, sixth from the left.

Pampa, about 1930, l. to r.: Matt Jennings,
Woody, and a friend, Kenneth Campbell.

The string band, Pampa, Texas, early 1930s:
Woody (with moustache) is number one.   Fifth
from left: Mary Jennings' brother, Matt.

On the road, 1930s.

California, 1939–40: Woody and Mary Guthrie
with Teeney, Sue, and Bill.

Woody in California, October, 1939.

CALIFORNIA

I N 1937, LIKE THOUSANDS OF OTHERS, Woody went to California; Mary and the girls were to remain with the family in Pampa until he could afford to send for them.

Woody's California experience shaped the rest of his life. It was out there that he wrote some of his best songs, among them the Dust Bowl Ballads. He became the voice of the Okies and Arkies, traveling up and down the West Coast, singing his songs on their behalf.

Back in Oklahoma, tales of the fruit valleys of California had seemed to promise paradise: jobs, warm weather, no dust.

"All of us would get together," Woody recalled, "in the little old shacks there in the Dust Bowl and we would talk about some place to go where we could get a piece of land or a little farm and get out of that dust and all that dust pneumonia and all that wind up there on the Texas plains. . . . They sat around and talked there for weeks and weeks, hated to give up what they worked there for fifty years and be born and raised and married on—and had their kids on this land.

"They owed thousands of dollars in debts and when they couldn't pay them, well naturally they come down with the mortgage and took their land.

"These people just got up and hit this road with moderately little belongings, things they thought they would need. They didn't have the money for gasoline.

"They heard about the land of California where you sleep

outdoors all night and work all day in the big fruits and make enough money to get by on and live decent on."

Those hopes and aspirations were embodied in a song called *California Blues:*

Going to California and sleeping out every night
'Cause the Oklahoma women just ain't treating you right
And I would rather drink muddy water and sleep in a
    hollow log
Than to be down in Texas treated like a dirty dog.
Them California waters taste like cherry wine
As the Georgia waters taste like turpentine.

California Blues, especially as recorded by Jimmy Rodgers, "the yodeling brakeman," swept the South and Southwest. The record became more than a best seller—it made converts.

"That record went," said Woody, "through Oklahoma . . . Texas, Georgia, Alabama, Tennessee, Mississippi and Kansas. I have seen hundreds and hundreds of people gang around an electric phonograph and listen to . . . that song.

"And they'd punch each other in the ribs with their elbows —'Boy, there's a place to go. That old boy is singing the truth. Listen to him sing! I'm telling you it makes me want to pick up right now and leave—"California waters taste like cherry wine; sleep out every night." ' "

The California peach and apricot growers, seeking a large and cheap labor supply, circulated handbills throughout the Dust Bowl, promising what they never intended to deliver: "Eight hundred wanted, Come on out! Get the jobs while they're hot!" But there were no 800 jobs when they arrived, and thousands of people traveled thousands of miles in broken-down jalopies only to suffer bitter disappointment. The trek to California was a series of hardships: hunger, exposure to blistering heat and numbing cold, and encounters with police and railroad bulls.

74

As crowds of down-and-outers, riding freight trains and bumming rides on the highway, arrived in towns along the way, police would line the men up at the railroad station to buy tickets for as far as their money could carry them. It was an ironic situation: nothing to eat and forced to buy tickets to some place they didn't know or want to know! Woody wrote: "It was highly unsanitary to be out of work. In most towns all over the country it is a jailhouse offense to be unemployed and they enforced that when they took a notion. Having money was all that counted. They don't ask you how you got it, just so you got the do-re-mi, that's the main thing." And he sang:

Lots of folks back East, they say,
Leavin' home every day
Beatin' a hot old dusty way
To the California line.

'Cross the desert sands they roll
Gettin' out of the old Dust Bowl,
Think they're a-comin' to a Sugar Bowl,
But here's what they find—

The police at the port of entry say
You're number fourteen thousand for today—Oh!

Chorus
If you ain't got the do-re-mi, Boys
If you ain't got the do-re-mi
You better go back to beautiful Texas,
Oklahoma, Kansas, Georgia, Tennessee.

California is a garden of Eden
A paradise to live in or see.
But believe it or not you won't find it's so hot
If you ain't got the do-re-mi!

75

When Woody got to California, he saw it all:

■　Hundreds and thousands of families . . . under railroad bridges, . . . in beat-up houses made out of tow sacks and old dirty rags and corrugated iron that they got out of dumps . . . and old orange crates—I couldn't believe it.

They had a little old spring of water . . . to do their wash in, to shave in, wash their teeth in, drink from and even for sewerage disposal.　Three or four hundred families trying to get along on a stream of water that wasn't any bigger than the stream of water that comes from your fau-
■ cet!

But no matter how badly the Dust Bowlers were treated in California, they knew it was worse back home.

■　We remembered the old tractor . . . covered up by dust, the dust standing up on top of the barn; and looking out across that dead sea of dust.　And we said, "No mister, I would rather be in jail here than setting down there on that farm."　. . . People from Oklahoma that had worked hard all their lives and split walnut and oak timber, drilled oil wells, picked that cotton, raised crops.　When they got to California and heard everybody calling them just the "Dust Bowl Refugees," why, they didn't know exactly what to do about it.　They didn't know what the people meant when they called somebody else a "refugee."

They walked down the highways, carried their shoes in their hands, and walked across the desert with blisters all over their feet, 2,000 miles, trying to find a job of work.

We had always been taught to believe that these 48 states that is called the United States was absolutely free country and that anybody who took a notion to get up and go any- where in these 48 states, could, without anybody else ask- ing him a whole bunch of questions or trying to keep him from going where he started out to go.

76

Well, the native California sons and daughters, I will admit, had a lot to be proud of. They had their ancestors that come in on the old covered wagons and discovered oil, gold and silver, and built California to quite a wonderful empire.

But they hadn't built quite a wonderful enough empire. They needed more and more people to pick their fruit. But they looked down for some reason on the people that come in there from other states to do that kind of ■ work.

In *Dust Bowl Refugee* Woody tells of the hard life of the migrant workers, wandering from job to job.

> I'm a Dust Bowl refugee,
> Just a Dust Bowl refugee
> From that Dust Bowl to the Peach Bowl.
> Now the peach fuzz is killing me.
>
> 'Cross the mountains to the sea,
> Come the wife and kids and me,
> It's a hot old dusty highway
> For the Dust Bowl refugees.
>
> . . . .
>
> Yes we wander and we work
> In your crops and in your fruit,
> Like the whirlwinds on the desert
> That's the Dust Bowl refugees.

Woody came to know the life of a refugee as he traveled west, an old mandolin slung on his back, his pockets bulging with brushes and tubes of paint. He had gotten a ride out of Pampa in a blinding snowstorm mixed with black dust. Somehow he managed to survive that first freezing night by spending his last dollar on a movie and fifty-cent flop in Amarillo. Then a few oil hands heading further west picked him up, only to abandon him in another town when he wandered off to look for a sign-painting job.

Woody had always paid his way with his music or painting, never seeking charity. Now, for the first time in his life, he had to panhandle for his meals. He knocked on doors of the well heeled when driven by weakness and hunger, but often found that poor families, who had nothing to lose, were more charitable. And so he traveled on, sometimes by thumb, more often by freight.

Riding the western train at fifty miles an hour, Woody saw the fertile farmland change to dry, corroded wasteland. Sometimes the train rattled across canyon beds cut by rivers and gullies. The clay earth was sometimes red, sometimes yellow. Flat-topped cliffs and earth-colored hills stood sharply etched against the distant sky like lonely sentinels in the endless desert. Once in a while they would follow the highway, the men on the train waving to the people speeding by in their cars.

After the deserts of the Southwest, the fertile valleys of California looked like Gardens of Eden, with fruit hanging from the trees, "groceries all over the ground, and people all over everything." Accustomed to the dustbowl, Woody was overwhelmed by the bright colors and delicious smells which permeated the air. The earth was rich, damp and green. But all around him were signs which read: "Fruit—see, but don't pick it" or "Fruit, beat it," or "Keep Out."

The fruit was rotting on the ground, enough to feed every hungry mouth from Maine to Seattle. Highway 99 was crowded with hitchhikers eager for an honest day's work and yet, there were the signs saying "No Work Here"—and the trees heavy with ripe fruit. The growing labor unrest was working against both the fruit grower and the Dust Bowler.

A young Japanese-American picked up Woody on the highway and drove him as far as the Mission Plaza in Los

78

Angeles. The fog was rolling in from the ocean. Red and green neon lights flickered on and off, hazily illuminating hotels, honky tonks, hamburger joints, laundries, and shops of all kinds.

Woody walked the city streets—through a few tunnels, past the Lincoln Heights jail, and down the San Fernando Road, looking for an odd job. He hadn't eaten in some time. Finally, a little greasy spoon joint gave him a meal, a takeout lunch, and a quarter in return for mopping the floor down with scalding lye water.

It was midnight and raining when Woody went to the railroad yards to hop a freight for the town of Turlock, where he had relatives. A train was heading out. "I let the train get too fast a start," Woody wrote years later, "and grabbed a sealed reefer that I couldn't get into, so had to hang on the outside between two cars into Bakersfield, as the wind was too strong and too cold on top. I unfroze my hands by putting a handkerchief over them and blowing my hot breath into them, because they got stiff and I couldn't use any of my fingers, and they was turning loose from the iron ladder. That was the closest to the 6 x 3 that I've ever been."

The trip turned out to be well worth the risk. Woody found his relatives and a temporary home in Turlock. He and his cousin, a carpenter, drove back and forth to the gold fields further north around Sonora, doing odd jobs. One day, Jeff the fiddling deputy and Allene the accordionist drove up from Texas and moved in, together with Jack, another cousin, who followed the rodeos as a guitar picker and yodeler. The exact reaction of the California relatives to this invasion was not recorded for posterity, but before long, the Texas-Oklahoma contingent moved back south to Los Angeles, hoping to find work and pick up extra cash playing in local bars and beaneries.

For six weeks they worked in the kitchen of Strangler Lewis' Monterey Lounge on Brand Boulevard in Glendale, just outside Los Angeles. The restaurant employed six dish-

79

washers, one of whom was Woody.   One day he ruined a tub full of aluminum, sizzling-steak skillets by trying to clean them with lye. . . .   "After a hot argument with the big chef, I turned Monterey Lounge back to the company."

Cousin Jack and Woody decided to go into the music business.   They bought an old Model-T Truck, draped it with a worn-out harness, and drove all around Hollywood, Pasadena and Burbank.

They appeared at a big Radio Stars Jamboree at the Shrine Auditorium in Los Angeles and were hired for a week's work at the Grand Theater in Long Beach.   They received $2.50 each a day, and $4 for the car, which was painted with advertising signs saying "Headed For The Grand."

That was a springboard for better things.   They auditioned for station KFVD in Los Angeles, and got a fifteen-minute daily spot in the morning hours.

"Our songs were hillybilly," Woody recalled, "cowboy, religious, farm country work songs; songs about the boxcars, the boats, mines that caved in.   One favorite was the *Ship That Never Returned:*

One summer day when the wave was rippled
By the softest, gentlest breeze
Did a ship set sail with a cargo laden
For a port beyond the seas.

There were sweet farewells, there were loving signals
While a form was not yet discerned.
Tho' they knew it not, twas a solemn parting
For the ship that never returned.

Chorus
Did she ever return?   No she never returned
Her fate is yet unlearned.
Tho' for years and years there were fond ones watching
Yet the ship she never returned.

80

. . . and songs about children left orphans by sick mothers and drunkard fathers. We sung old songs, dust and dirt storms, floods, car wrecks, bad highways, fast horses, slow lovers and fast courters, away to the hills and the sunny mountain side." Like Jimmy Rodgers, Woody yodeled as he sang *Foggy Mountain Top,* a song made popular by the Carter Family:

> If I was on some foggy mountain top
> Tell you what I'd do.
> (I'd) Sing this song to the whole wide world
> Little gal that I'd love so true.
>
> If I had a ticket to heaven up above
> Upon the sky so blue
> I'd give it away for your true love
> On the old foggy mountain with you.

After the postcards started pouring in from listeners, the station gave them a second fifteen-minute program at midnight, in addition to the morning show. Woody and Jack were a hit. The only problem, as usual, was money.

The radio station paid them a big dollar a day, which hardly covered getting to and from the studio. To get by, Jack and Woody hustled saloons, Skid Row, and the clip joints. They sang on the movie lots, making friends among show people.

For a while they continued, hoping that the daily exposure on the air would be good publicity or, as Woody put it, "give us enough prestige to ask for a two-dollar guarantee for six hours." Jack lasted a few months and then hit the road again, preferring to take his chances in harvest towns, fairs, and rodeos.

For a few weeks Woody did the programs by himself, and then got a new partner, "Lefty Lou" Crissman.

Roy Crissman had come from the Missouri Ozarks grazing

81

country, with his wife and their two daughters, Mary Ruth and "Lefty Lou." Lefty Lou was a tall thin-faced farm girl with a rough, husky voice. After a few meals of pinto beans with ham hock, a few jugs, and "a few days of backyard singing," they decided to team up together.

→For almost two years Lefty Lou and Woody sang over KFVD every morning and night. She fainted under the piano a minute or so before the first program but after the initial shock, performed like a veteran. They received thousands of letters during those years from fans who were troubled, or old and sick, from people who wanted to hear the truth about their hard times.

Around this time, Woody's first social protest songs appeared, gathered together in a mimeographed booklet entitled *Woody and Lefty Lou's Favorite Old Time Hillbilly Songs* (1937).

"Lefty and me sung songs," he wrote, "pointing fingers to the rich and lazy homes of idle dreamers, to the offices of phonies, to the padded hotels of racketeers, the big birds, the land grabbers, oil stealers, landlords, the mean cops, the drunken sheriffs, the bad boss, the stealing foreman, the whole mess of people forced to live by fear and greed under the monopoly setup."

They traveled all over Los Angeles a hundred times, picked up songs from every street and alley, listened to what people were saying on the docks and fishing boats, and watched ships leave for Japan loaded with iron and oil. Japan had intensified her war on China in 1937, and there was rising sentiment against any American trade that helped support her aggression.

Woody had long since passed the dollar-a-day mark. The station was now paying twenty dollars a week apiece for him and his partner. Their fans grew in number and soon they were receiving offers from medicine, insurance, and hair-dye companies. Even Hollywood studios were making offers of "a hundred or so a week." At twenty-five Woody Guthrie had become a radio personality.

82

At one point, Woody and Lefty Lou quit KFVD to broadcast for a drug company on XELO, in Tijuana, Mexico. Now they were in the big money: $75 per week—$45 for Woody, $30 for Lefty Lou. Allene and Jack came down to help out on the program, traveling over the border every day to the station at Tijuana.

The program proved to be nothing but a pack of trouble. First, there were censorship problems. Woody's recollection is a gem:

■ The radio agent . . . gave us friendly talks about not singing any song that took sides with anybody, anywhere, on any fight, argument, idea, or belief, from a religious, scientific, political, legal or illegal point of view, nor from any point of thought that would cause anybody, anywhere, to act, think, move or perform any motion in any direction, to agree or disagree with any one single word of any one single song or conversation, joke, tall tale, that we performed, dressed, or even thought about in the radio studios which was in a little blockhouse on a hill a mile or so away from
■ the smells of Tijuana.

As the last straw, they discovered that the radio agent was pocketing money on the sly from the sponsors for every letter Woody and Lefty Lou received from their fans! To make things worse, the Chief of Police found out they were working in Mexico without proper permits. Of course, he was perfectly willing to ignore the illegalities in return for "mordida" (the Mexican term for "bite")—or kickback. Woody and the rest of the family refused and were promptly fired.

Woody and Lefty Lou went back to KFVD for another two months and quit again. Out of work, the Crissman family and Woody went down to the peach country and set up their tent along the Sacramento River.

→Although it was peach-picking season, carloads of good peaches were rotting on the ground. No one was being hired to pick them. Big deputies guarded the orchards with rifles and sawed-off shotguns, but Woody and his friends sneaked across the river at night, filled big pasteboard boxes full of Alberta peaches, and distributed them among the hundreds of unemployed fruit pickers.

Mothers would sit up a whole night boiling peaches in huge cans, fanning the little fires of smoking rags to keep them going, while battling the bugs, gnats, and flies that swarmed in from the river bed, drawn by the stench of rotting fruit blowing in from the orchards.

Living on fish, wild rabbits, and stolen peaches, Woody and Lefty Lou sang in the camps of migrant workers along the Sacramento River, and in nearby saloons for tips. One day they had an argument about Lou flirting with a gold miner, and the team broke up. It was not the first time they had quarreled, but it was the last.

Woody had many an opportunity to know the camps of the migrants. In 1938, while he was living in Los Angeles, he caught a freight one day and headed out for Redding, California, at a bend of the Sacramento River where the government was about to build a dam. According to rumors 2500 workers were needed. Within a short time, eight thousand people turned up. Several thousand set up a "jungle camp" a mile or so out of town to wait for the work to begin.

Woody arrived one morning in the company of at least a hundred men, all carrying their bed rolls and bundles. As he walked along the street he could hear singing and playing coming from the open doors of the saloons. He stopped to play and sing his longest, saddest ballads in various spots along the way. Such old songs were loved by the Dust Bowlers, for they were reminders of the homes and farms they had left behind. By the end of the day Woody had collected enough money to buy himself a new shirt and pants. With twenty cents change in his pocket, he headed out for the jungle camp.

It was bigger than the town itself. People had rigged up shelters of all kinds out of old car-fenders, wagon sheets, and flattened tin cans. The kids played around old, smelly quilts hung up like tents. Every kind of bug, tick, gnat, and cater-pillar was crawling around, flying overhead, and biting human flesh.

The men sat around playing cards or whittling. The women rocked their babies, nursing as many children as they had milk for.

Many young people wandered around playing and singing to guitars and banjos. Of these, two sisters, one fourteen and the other twelve, attracted the most attention. Every evening just at sundown they would bring a guitar out, tune up, try a few chords and begin to sing—not so much to entertain the people of the camp as to keep their baby brother happy. As soon as the baby heard the music he would climb into one sis-ter's lap and kick his feet contentedly to the rhythm of the music.

Woody listened to them every night from a distance. He enjoyed their quiet, plain singing, the feeling of the rest and peace that it gave him. When he sang in saloons, he had to bawl out his songs to be heard above the raucous noise of drunks and the scraping of chairs on the floor. The girls' songs were not meant to stimulate the listener mentally, mor-ally, or sexually. Perhaps they did something much better and harder to do, Woody thought to himself. "It cleared your head up, that's what it done, caused you to fall back and let your draggy bones rest and your muscles go limber like a cat's."

People went about their chores as they listened, but no one talked above a whisper. Those two girls were helping every-one by singing songs about their lives and hard times. They gave those weary people hope that they would come through it all in good shape.

Woody finally talked to the two sisters. "I like the soft way you play. I've got to be loud when I play in saloons. . . ."

Woody took down his guitar and joined the girls, who were singing *Columbus Stockade*. Without interrupting them, he put his ear down to the guitar strings, tuned himself in, and picked out the melody while the girls played the bass chords and second part. The crowd loved the sound of the two guitars playing together. It was the music they were raised on and loved the most.

> Go and leave me if you want to
> Never let me cross your mind
> In your heart you love another
> Leave me darling I don't mind.

> Way down in a lonesome jail house
> Left me here to lose my mind
> Thinkin' about the time we parted
> I was yours and you was mine.

Woody and the two sisters sang song after song. The audience drifted in out of the shadows, and grew bigger and bigger. Late that night the men who had been drinking and gambling in the saloons came back to the camp. About twenty-five or thirty men, yelling, cussing, and kicking buckets and pots in their way, came running down the trail to where the singing was going on. When they got to the clearing they quieted down and took seats on the ground. Everybody sat so still you could hear the "lightning bugs turn their lights on and off." The little girls sang on and on. And there was rest in the camp that night.

> It takes a worried man to sing a worried song
> It takes a worried man to sing a worried song
> It takes a worried man to sing a worried song
> I'm worried now but I won't be worried long.

> I went across the river and I lay down to sleep
> I went across the river and I lay down to sleep
> I went across the river and I lay down to sleep
> When I woke up I had shackles on my feet.

Twenty-one links of chain around my legs
Twenty-one links of chain around my legs
Twenty-one links of chain around my legs
And on each link the initial of my name.

Woody returned to Los Angeles and KFVD, this time all alone. He rented a house with his younger brother, George, who had hitchhiked from Texas to California to take a job as a clerk in a big market. George paid the rent and Woody paid the other bills. Playing at night joints, Woody saved enough money to send for Mary and their two little girls, Sue and Teeny.

Woody continued to write songs about conditions in the migrant jungles. The sight of "people living hungrier than rats and dirtier than dogs in the land of the sun and a valley of night breezes" set him to composing song after song. He was not yet thirty, but people were beginning to know his name and his songs.

By the end of the 1930's the entire country was ablaze with the organizing activities of the new Congress of Industrial Organizations (CIO). Originating as a committee formed by dissident leaders within the American Federation of Labor, it was now a separate entity, organizing millions of formerly unorganized workers on an industry-wide basis. There were long and dreadful strikes in heavy industry and endless tie-ups by longshoremen in East and West Coast ports. Thugs were brought in to break the strikes, reprisals followed, and violence on the picket line became a daily occurrence. Heads were broken and blood spilled on the streets, but a sense of unity and strength was growing among the working class. They believed they could improve their own lot through political action. So they took to the streets, and in meetings, demonstrations and hunger marches, made their demands known. (Much of what they demanded then was later enacted into law and eventually taken for granted.)

The political atmosphere was charged with talk of

revolution. Many believed that only the most fundamental changes could bring relief to the country, and the Communists, who spoke openly in these terms, attracted many to their ranks.

Woody's songs and radio programs soon brought him to the attention of both progressives and radicals, but although he aligned himself with them, he was too much of an individualist ever to become a doctrinaire party man. "I may not necessarily be a Communist," he once wrote, "but I've never been out of the Red!"

It was inevitable that Woody would associate himself with the radical left and the trade union movement. The optimism that permeated the activities of the political left was strongly reflected in his songs. In 1939 he put out a mimeographed collection of songs entitled *On A Slow Train Through California,* his first protest songs, among which were early versions of *Do, Re, Mi* and *Talking Dust Bowl Blues,* two of the best songs about the Dust Bowl. The blues number became a particular favorite:

Back in Nineteen twenty-seven,
I had a little farm
And I called that heaven.
The price is up and the rain come down
And I hauled my crops all into town.
I got the money,
Bought clothes and groceries
Fed the kids and raised a family.

Rain quit and the wind got high
And a black old dust storm filled the sky,
And I swapped my farm for a Ford machine,
And I poured it full of gasoline.
I started rocking and rolling.
Over the mountains out towards
The Old Peach Bowl. . . .

Woody observed, "I didn't sing in any of my songs the whole answer, nor the real answer, because I didn't know about unions, nor about Communist organizers, nor about the People's Daily World, nor about the Daily Worker, nor about the AF of L, nor the CIO, nor about anything, except the looks in the eyes and faces of these seas and oceans of people living like things in the dark jungle."

Although Woody's criticism was aimed increasingly at the social and economic institutions bound up with the system, he was never a political pamphleteer. His songs of social protest were always warm, human, and personal. The people in his songs are flesh and blood, and the situations the stuff of life. No matter how grim the subject, Woody always found the humor embedded somewhere to give balance and hope.

Woody's political values matured as he met West Coast radicals and union leaders. At KFVD he met the singer Cisco Houston, who was to become his lifelong and closest friend, and Ed Robbin, a news commentator for the *People's World*. Soon he was writing a daily column called *Woody Sez,* which he illustrated with his own sketches.

One day an actor named Will Geer came to the radio studio to see him. He was working in Pare Lorentz' *Fight For Life,* a film about the Chicago Maternity Center, and they needed two pregnant women. Woody's wife and his cousin Amalee qualified; both women were just about ready to give birth. (Shortly afterward Bill, the third young Guthrie, was born.) Like other members of the film colony, Will was concerned with the fate of the migrant workers flocking to California—a concern that translated itself into benefit performances on their behalf. Woody would come along and lend his talents. They sang at fancy house parties in plush homes all around Beverly Hills, Hollywood, Los Angeles and San Pedro, drank fine wines, and nibbled cheese and crackers "to win the passionate souls of Hollywood Business men."

Woody and Will Geer rode back and forth over the mountains in a '31 Chevy, singing and making speeches at union forums, rallies, picnics, and on picket lines. They shared the stage with political and labor figures of every description. No one could resist their songs; strikers, police, and even hired thugs would be caught up by the music, breaking for the moment the vicious cycle of violence and counterviolence.

In addition, Will and Woody organized "educational tours" for the mutual benefit of Hollywood people and migrant workers. Caravans from Hollywood traveled to Okie and Arkie camps to see conditions at first hand. Then they hauled strikers and their families over to Hollywood to stage country dances. As the dancers whirled through their sets and the fiddlers stomped out the rhythm, the warmth and the fighting quality of the dispossessed people of the Dust Bowl was keenly felt by all who watched.

Woody had always believed in the power of music to influence the heart and mind. He saw the labor movement as a weapon against "hate marauders and profit grabbers"; but the movement needed songs to help it grow and he criticized certain left-wing intellectual leaders for being out of touch with the rank and file in this respect:

"Some are consciously trying to keep singing out of the people's throats, and some are just too neurotically bookish, too mossyback, too scared, or too timid, that they feel that this rawkish singing actually lowers the dignity of the meeting place."

He also had confidence that the people themselves would compose their own songs!

■ And the best part of the whole story is not about me nor about my mouth harp nor my guitar, but it is about several thousand folks all the way across the country that are grabbing pencils and tablets and writing down stories set to easy old tunes, everytime they see a gun, a billy stick, a piece of lead pipe smash into the face of a picket, or a striker, or a speaker along the streets. And the cops all knew how easy,

how fiery, a song and a tune spreads, how long a song
■ echoes around in the streets and valleys.

Woody believed implicitly in the power of songs to stir
human beings:

■　I can show you a dozen clippings I've got here where the
cops, even the hired thugs, the vigilantes, joined in and
hummed and laughed with the songs.　They did not laugh
at the pamphlets, they did not hum the editorials, they did
not dance the factual charts and graphs, nor whistle the
proofs, affidavits, the warrants, the court papers, the
printed word in any form.　It was the deep running personal sentiments of those songs that caused the paid gang-
■ ster to lay down his oily gun.

Wartime, 1942: Woody plays for the troops.

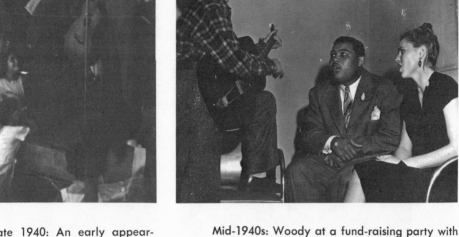

Late 1940: An early appearance at a benefit for veterans of the Abraham Lincoln Brigade, a company of American volunteers fighting the Franco forces in the Spanish Civil War. (Photo by George Gilbert)

Mid-1940s: Woody at a fund-raising party with heavyweight champion Joe Louis and folksinger Hally Wood.

Some of the Almanac Singers in the early 1940s, l. to r.: Woody, Mill Lampell, Bess Lomax Hawes, Pete Seeger, Arthur Stern, Sis Cunningham.

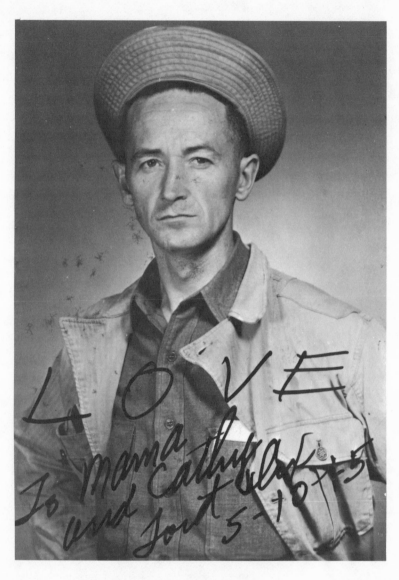

1945: Woody in the U.S.
Army, Fort Dix, New Jersey.

NEW YORK

I N THE EARLY 1940's New York was the scene of political and artistic ferment. Though the worst of the Depression was over, there were violent strikes and demonstrations for relief and jobs. The fight for social security, social justice, and racial equality involved not only those directly affected, but many professional people and artists as well. The war in Europe was threatening to engulf America and anti-war demonstrations and meetings were held everywhere.

Activities of all kinds flourished. The Works Progress Administration (WPA) art projects, supported by the federal government since the early Depression years, had generated a new vitality. There was experimentation with new ideas and forms in theater, music, dance, fine arts, and literature. Professional artists were reaching out beyond narrow traditional confines. Conservatory-trained musicians were listening to and even trying to emulate the "hot jazz" of that time. At the many fund-raising parties for political and social causes, at the famous rent parties held to help friends in need, musicians reared in the classics got a second education from "black-butt" boogie-woogie pianists. White and black gathered uptown at the Harlem night spots—at the famous Savoy to watch the dancers and, if you had the money, at the Cotton Club to hear Cab Calloway.

Onto this scene came another kind of music: folk music,

97

the sound of rural America. City youth listened enthusiastically to country singers coming in from the trouble spots of the nation. There was Aunt Molly Jackson, her sister Sarah Ogan, and her half brother Jim Garland, all strike leaders from Harlan County, Kentucky, where coal miners had been fighting since the 1920's to organize an honest union. Huddie Ledbetter ("Leadbelly"), the complete black musician, played his twelve-string guitar and sang gut-bucket blues, spirituals, sukey-jump tunes, and work songs from the Deep South. Their voices and country-singing style seemed crude by big-city standards, but audiences were turned on by the raw sound and the ring of truth in their songs. They sang of life, not as idealized in slick Tin-Pan Alley songs, but as it really was, in all its stark reality.

The times called for a new kind of popular music, one which would echo and inspire the rebellious upsurge, the new ideas crying out for expression. Songs were needed also to voice the sense of common purpose which had been steadily emerging since the early Depression years. The hardships of that period had drawn people together, stirring up a feeling of kinship among millions across the nation.

Woody Guthrie was to lead the way in the creation of a new significant popular music, rooted in the rural past and refurbished for the needs of the urban present. He took traditional American backwoods tunes, molded them to his purpose, and wrote new words. He had learned them from his ballad-singing mother, his blues-singing father, Uncle Jeff, Cousin Jack Guthrie, and other relatives. He picked up songs from the string bands he had traveled with, and from the recordings. The "yodeling brakeman," Jimmy Rodgers, who introduced the blues to country music, and the Carter Family, who recorded more than three hundred songs between 1927 and 1940, made a lasting impression on country musicians. Woody used to play their disks (and many others) until the grooves were worn out, learning guitar style and harmony for use in his own work.

98

Those were prolific years of writing and performing, of meeting people, of intellectual challenge. The recordings of the *Dust Bowl Songs* and the *Bonneville Dam Songs* and the publication of his autobiography *Bound For Glory* in 1943, were products of this period.

Woody came to New York for the first time in 1940, at Will Geer's invitation. Despite his reputation as a singer and song writer, despite his popularity with the labor movement, he was unable to earn a decent living by doing what he wanted to do in California. Five dollars or three dollars earned at meetings and demonstrations—if he received anything at all—barely covered the expenses of traveling, let alone food and rent for the family. It was the old story.

One day Woody, Mary, and the three children, Sue, Teeny and Bill, took off from Los Angeles in their ancient, beatup car for Pampa, Texas, where Mary's folks lived. Once again, Mary and the children stayed behind in Pampa, while Woody went on alone to Konawa, Oklahoma, to see his brother Roy. The thirty-five dollars he borrowed from Roy paid for the rest of his trip eastward to New York City.

In February Woody made his first major appearance in New York, singing at Mecca Temple for the Spanish Refugees Relief Fund to help victims of the fascist Franco regime. But more important was a midnight concert given at a Broadway theater in March to raise money for the California migrant workers. The *Grapes of Wrath,* John Steinbeck's powerful indictment of the Okies' plight, had been published a year before, and the cause of the Dust Bowl people had become the cause of the progressives. Will Geer, at whose house Woody was then staying, was the Show's MC. It was on this occasion that Woody first met and shared the stage with some of the leading folk singers—the young Pete Seeger, Leadbelly, bluesman Josh White, and singer-actor Burl Ives. Woody was, Seeger recalls, "a little short fellow with a western hat and boots, in blue jeans and needing a shave, spinning out stories and singing songs that he had made up himself. His manner was

99

laconic, offhand, as though he didn't much care if the audience was listening or not. I became a friend of his, and he became a big piece of my education."

Woody wandered the streets of New York, rode the subways, gaped at the skyscrapers and wrote his impressions in a column for *The Daily Worker*.

■ I'm still a-ramblin' 'round old New York trying to find me a job of work. I been here for about three weeks a-walkin' around these old cold streets. Sometimes up and sometimes down, sometimes lost in a hole in the ground.

One runs east, two go west, and I wonder how to catch the best. Six go south, and nine run north, and you dang sure get your nickels worth.

You put a nickel in the slot and grab you a train that's good and hot, sail out down a hole in the ground and ride that train across this town.

People push and people jam, the jammedest jam I mean what am. You walk, you nudge and squirm and fall, and get up against that cement wall, and ooze and duck and spar and strain and they shove you into the wrong dam train. . . .

I believe there is more of New York underground than on top. New York is funny. The streets are half a block long and three blocks wide. And the town is half a town
■ wide, and three towns high.

The human ravages of the Depression were already visible down on the Bowery in New York's lower East Side.

■ The Skiddiest Row I ever seen is the Bowery in New York City. I didn't know human beings could get so broke, hungry, and so dirty and ragged, and still remain alive. The wine they drink must come out through the pores of their skin and get the disease germs so drunk they can't organize. . . . Guys passed out drunk on the cement steps of the stores and banks. Draped around the light

100

posts, slumped over the fire plugs, and sleeping around up against the bronze statues in the parks—and any one of them statues cost enough to feed a man a solid year. If you happen to have the notion in your head that there aint no work to be done except to spend all of your money on bombs—I suggest that you take a look at Skid Row and in-
■ vest your money in making men out of bums.

Woody met many people during the New York years. In the small, but closely knit folk-song world, he found his most intimate friends. He wrote about them with tender affection:

■ Aunt Molly Jackson and her relatives from Harlan County, Kentucky all come to Leadbelly's house almost every day. She would sing us an hour or two of Bloody Harlan County songs, of organizing the coal miners to beat the thugs of old Sheriff Blair. Molly told tales from her life as a mountaineer midwife, sung us the songs that she used to make the sweethearts lose their bashfulness and the older ones to be in body and action as quick, as funny, as limber and as wise as the younguns coming up. Molly is the woman Leadbelly. She is in her cotton apron what Leadbelly is in his bathrobe. She talks to him exactly as to her reflection in her mirror. He speaks back to her like the swamplands to the uplands, the same as his river would talk to her highest cliffrim. She loves him in the same half-jealous way that he loves her, because he sees and feels in Aunt Molly the woman who has found in her own voice
■ the same power on earth as he has found.

I am a union woman
Just as brave as I can be.
I do not like the bosses
And the bosses don't like me.

Join the CIO
Come join the C.I.O.

I was raised in Kentucky
In Kentucky borned and bred
And when I joined the Union
They called me a Rooshian Red.

When my husband asked the boss for a job
This is the words he said,
Bill Jackson I can't work you sir
Your wife's a Rooshian Red.

The bosses ride their big fine white horse
While we walk in the mud.
Their flag's the old red, white and blue
And ours is dipped in blood.

For Molly's sister he had a special regard:

■   Sarah Ogan is the wife of a Kentucky Coal Miner.   Her
man died with T.B. caused by working too long and too
hard in the mines.   Sarah's got 2 of the finest and best
children you ever seen.   A boy and a girl. . . .

She snuck in the Jail House through a hole in the rear
wall to bring secret notes and letters to Strikers that was in
Jail.   She went back under the mountain in a big black
coal shaft every night and stole a sack of coal to cook
meals for her kids and sick husband.   She met the sheriff,
and he said, "What ya got in that there sack, Sary?"   And
Sarah says, "It's so dark I dont know if it's lumps of coal or
rocks, sherf. . . ."   He says, "You dam shore better'd not
let me cetch you a stealin' that coal no more, Sary, I'll
throw you in jail shore as hell . . . dont let me cetch you
here no more."

"You'll cetch me right here again as quick as the kids get
hungry and when I get to a needin' some more coal, Sherf."

■   The Sherf rode on.

About another close friend, Woody wrote:

■ Earl Robinson is the boy that wrote the songs *Joe Hill, Abe Lincoln, Ballad for Americans,* and a raft of others. I heard 'em sung from coast to coast. . . .

If our gossipers up in the capital would learn to sing Earl's songs, and to make some laws like 'em, the war and the hard times would both end.

Here's to more guys like old Earl!

■ And less cops.

Will Geer, who had come to New York to play the leading role in the play, *Tobacco Road,* had remained one of Woody's oldest and closest friends. Woody wrote a thumbnail sketch of him:

■ Tobacco Road is closing in N.Y. after breaking all endurance records for hungry farmers and lady preachers. Will Geer is a farmer at heart. Studied plant husbandry in college. He's got him a big garden out here in the country. Pretty good at it, too. He's the only man I know of that knows these vegetables by their maiden names. He sticks his head out of the window and hollers about two dollars worth of Latin, and you know, them vegetables just come a running and jump in the stew pot. So if Will can't make a farm pay on Tobacco Road, the average dirt farmer

■ ain't got a chance.

But Woody admired few people in the whole wide world as much as Huddie Ledbetter. He lived with him, "studied," and worked with him. The period he lived in Leadbelly's small apartment in downtown New York was one of the great privileges and pleasures of his life. In October, 1940, I received a letter from Woody asking me to keep Leadbelly on the air on WNYC.

October 3, 1940

■ Howdy Mrs. 'Chenko—

You might be interested to know that Leadbelly and me have been working on a lot of things together and we'd like to have you hear them and arrange some programs in Adventures in Music—because I honestly believe that of all the living folk singers I've ever seen that Leadbelly is ahead of them all. I'm sure that lots of folks believe just the same way I do. There are others as great I reckon but I've never had the good luck to run onto them. There is Blind Lemon Jefferson, who to my notion put out the best blues in anybody's Blues Book when he made his One Dime Blues, and you can ask Alan Lomax and he will say that Blind Lemons One Dimes Blues is first on his list too. Huddie had the good fortune to study and travel with Blind Lemon and now I am lucky enough to study under Huddie which is to me one of New York's greatest pleasures. I argue that it is a mistake for the people in the radio world to leave Leadbelly out of the picture, its like leaving the alcohol out of the wine or leaving the spring out of the clock. You are one of the only persons that knows folk music good enough to realize what place Huddie holds and you know that it is wrong for the people of the air waves not to hear Huddie. I have been working with him now for several months and we have pretty well got the hang of how we ought to work together and I think that he will tell you that what really comes out of him mostly depends on who is working with him or enjoying it with him. Some radio experts will say that Huddie is too rough and so pass him up but I say that he is just too good and so they can't see it. Life hasn't been so smooth with Huddie and what makes him so good is that he simply wants to sing and tell how it has treated him, and what he has learned from it, and he wants to be honest about it, without any pretty put on. Huddie plays a little old $4 accordion and you can actually hear the sad note of his people ringing in the swamps and jungles and echoing in the Louisiana moss. And when you hear it you almost know that it's the sad and lonesome music of a people that can't even vote. But what they have been beat out of by votes

they've tried to win back with notes and to my way of thinking they've won it and will keep on winning it. Leadbelly ought to be kept on the radio regularly so that people would hear his name and then he could get more jobs and bookings and I know that he loves to work and needs it. I want to pat you on the back Henrietta for the help you've already been to Huddie and what you can
■ keep on doing. Take it easy but take it.

Woody Guthrie
10-3-1940
N.Y.N.YNYC. N.Y.n.y.ny

We gave Leadbelly a weekly fifteen-minute spot, and his program, *Folk Songs of America,* became one of the station's most popular features.

Through the efforts of the folklorist Alan Lomax, Woody received a contract to record his Dust Bowl Songs for RCA Victor. The only one written especially for the album was his long ballad, *Tom Joad,* set to the tune of *John Hardy,* a badman's song. All the others were earlier songs. At the same time, he continued to work on his column, *Woody Sez,* turning movie reviewer for one night after he had seen the film adaptation of *The Grapes of Wrath,* based on the Steinbeck novel.

■ Seen the pitcher last night, Grapes of Wrath, best cussed pitcher I ever seen. The Grapes of Wrath you know is about us a pullin' out of Oklahoma and Arkansas, and down south and out, and a driftin' around over the State of California, busted, disgusted, down and out, and a lookin' for work.

Shows you how come us to be that way. Shows the damn bankers, men that broke us and the dust that choked us, and comes right out in plain old English, and says what to do about it.

It says you got to get together and have some meetins,

105

and stick together and raise old billy hell till you get your job, and get your farm back, and your house and your chickens, and your groceries and your clothes, and your money back.

Go to see 'Grapes of Wrath' pardner, go to see it and don't miss. You was the star in that picture. Go and see your own self, and hear your own words and your own
■ songs.

Pete Seeger reports that Woody wrote *Tom Joad* one night in their apartment on the sixth floor of an East 4th Street tenement. Woody typed away, stopping every now and then to try the verse with the guitar, then type again. About one o'clock in the night, Pete went to sleep. When he awoke the next morning he found Woody asleep on the floor, huddled in his overcoat, an almost empty half-gallon jug of wine at his side. The finished ballad was near the typewriter.

Woody was invited to record his songs for the Library of Congress. The head of the Folklore Division, Alan Lomax, and his wife Elizabeth, interviewed him in Washington. These historic interviews were released two decades later in 1964 on Elektra Records and are among the most important documents of a significant period in American history.

Soon after his arrival in New York Woody began appearing on many radio programs. On CBS, he was guest on *Cavalcade of America, Back Where I Come From,* and the morning program originating from Washington, *School of the Air.* On WNYC, New York's municipal station, he was heard on *Adventures in Music,* one of the first programs dedicated to folk and non-Western music; on *The American Music Festivals;* and on Leadbelly's own weekly series, *Folk Songs of America.* He also broadcast a series for the Model Tobacco Company, for the handsome sum of $200 a week. After a month or so the company insisted that he stop writing his column for *The Daily Worker* and singing at leftist and union affairs. Woody stood firm and quit the program.

106

With the money he had earned he bought a car and headed down to Washington, D.C. There he joined Pete Seeger who was doing some work for the Library of Congress. "I quit my job," Pete recalled, "and we 'hitchhiked on credit' across the country." This was the first of many trips Woody and Pete were to make together during the next few years.

In 1941, again through the intervention of Alan Lomax, Woody was invited to Portland, Oregon, to discuss the possibility of writing some songs for a film on the work of the Bonneville Power Administration. Since 1918, when the Grand Coulee Dam was first proposed for the Columbia River, the Pacific Northwest had been a battleground between private and public power forces; the film, to be titled simply *The Columbia*, was to present the case for public power.

Woody put a down payment on a car, picked up Mary and their three children in Texas, and appeared one day in the Portland office of Stephen B. Kahn, the producer of *The Columbia*. "Woody showed up," recalled Mr. Kahn, "in a battered new car with broken windows, stained cushions, a blonde wife, three blonde children, and a guitar."

Soon after his arrival the car was reclaimed by the auto finance company for nonpayment of installments.

"He had a two-weeks growth of beard," mused Lloyd Hoff, an official of the Bonneville Power Administration, "and was chewing an apple. To those of us with sensitive noses, it was obvious that he was badly in need of a bath. He was free and easy in his conversation and completely uninhibited—but he was diamond sharp."

To hire Woody even for a short time required cutting through governmental red tape. Kahn sent Woody to see the top administrator himself, Dr. Paul J. Raver, hoping in that way to speed the process. He was right. Woody walked into Dr. Raver's office with his guitar, sang a number of his Dust Bowl Ballads, and was hired on the spot.

Kahn gave Woody some historical and background material on the Pacific Northwest, and for thirty days, the period of his employment, Woody wandered around, listening and watching. He saw the Bonneville and Grand Coulee Dams in construction, met and talked with Okies and other migrants who had come to work on the dams and eventually settle down.

"While he played songs for the office staff," Kahn wrote, "disrupting work in the process, Woody preferred to meet with the working people on the dams, the docks, and the roads, and in the bars. He had an endless array of anecdotes and a free and easy manner that made him at home wherever he went."

"The Pacific Northwest," Woody wrote a few years later, "is one of my favorite spots."

■ The Pacific Northwest has got mineral mountains, it's got chemical deserts, it's got rough-run canyons. It's got hills out of six colors of green, cliffs five shades of shadows and stickers the eight tones of hell. I pulled my shoes on and walked out of every one of those Pacific Northwest mountain towns drawing pictures in my mind and listening to poems and songs and words faster to come and dance in
■ my ears than I could ever get them wrote down.

In a small cubicle in the basement of the Bonneville Dam Administration building, Woody thumped out tunes on his battered guitar and pecked out the words on a department typewriter, turning out an astounding stream of songs. But it was not until 1948 that *The Columbia,* the film for which he had written them, was finally finished. Of the twenty-six original songs, only seven were incorporated into the sound track.

In April of 1966 when Woody was in Brooklyn State Hospital, Department of Interior Secretary Stewart L. Udall awarded him the Conservation Service Award in recognition of the work done twenty-five years earlier for the Bonneville Dam Administration. Besides the award, the Department

108

named an electric power facility in his honor. The 12,000 kilowatt Woody Guthrie Substation, a joint project of the Bonneville Power Administration and the Hood River Electric Cooperative, is nestled among the orchards of the valley between the snowy cap of Mount Hood and the fast-flowing Columbia River.

When the substation name was announced in 1966, a flurry of protests arose from local people, many of whom had never heard of Woody. Secretary Udall stood firm, and after a while the complaints ceased.

"I never heard of Woody Guthrie until the Bonneville people told us they wanted to name the substation for him," confessed Willard I. Johnson, manager of the Hood River Electric Cooperative. "I wasn't happy at all." But after hearing Woody's songs, he changed his mind. "I'm proud of the name. Since the Hood River is without a doubt one of the most beautiful areas in the nation, what could better typify the dreams he had for everybody?"

This Land Is Your Land, Pastures of Plenty, Roll On Columbia and *Talking Columbia,* were not only among Woody's finest songs; they were a paean of praise to the monumental beauty of his country—to its magnificent rivers, towering mountains, and fertile green valleys. He envisioned the Pacific Northwest as a symbol of America's opportunities and riches in which every citizen could participate and prosper.

This Land Is Your Land is known to millions all over America. But Woody wrote an earlier, more powerful version, called *God Blessed America For Me,* and some of the verses almost indicate a parody of Irving Berlin's *God Bless America:*

This land is your land, this land is my land
From California to the New York Island,
From the Redwood Forest, to the Gulf Stream waters,
God blessed America for me.

. . . .

As I went walking that ribbon of highway
And saw above me that endless skyway,
And saw below me the golden valley, I said:
God blessed America for me.

. . . .

Was a big high wall there that tried to stop me
A sign was painted said: Private Property,
But on the back side it didn't say nothing—
God blessed America for me.

. . . .

One bright sunny morning in the shadow of the steeple
By the Relief office I saw my people—
As they stood hungry, I stood there wondering if
God blessed America for me.

Later he changed the last line and substituted "This land was
made for you and me." In 1946, a mimeographed pamphlet
entitled *Ten Songs for Two Bits* included the following:

Nobody living can ever stop me
As I go walking my Freedom Highway.
Nobody living can make me turn back,
This land was made for you and me.

Back in New York after the Northwest trip, Woody joined
the newly-formed Almanac Singers, a group of folk singers
that included Pete Seeger and Lee Hays, a former Arkansas
preacher.

It had been a long, tiring trek back by freight car and
thumb, and Woody was in low spirits: Mary had left him on
the West Coast, this time for good. She was a loyal wife, but
she had had all she could take, trailing Woody cross-country
with three small children, and being constantly plagued by
money problems. Besides, they belonged to two different
110

worlds; Mary Jennings and Woody Guthrie disagreed on too many issues, including the upbringing of the children, to keep the marriage together. They were divorced some time later.

No sooner had Woody set foot in New York than the Almanacs excitedly asked him, "How about coming west with us?" Woody scratched his head, "I just came from there, but I don't mind if I join up with you."

In the next few days before they left, the Almanacs earned a few extra dollars by recording their first two albums of folk songs, *Sodbuster Ballads* and *Deepsea Shanties*. They bought a nine-year old gasoline-eating Buick for $125.00 and stashed away just enough money to get them to booking number one—the first of many.

On that first trip the Almanacs appeared before the automobile workers in Detroit and a dozen CIO unions in Chicago, Milwaukee, and Denver. In San Francisco they were coolly received by the militant longshoremen's union headed by Australian-born Harry Bridges.

"What the hell is a bunch of hillbilly singers coming in here for?" they complained. "We got work to do!" Pete Seeger still recalls the deafening applause after they had sung Woody's *Union Maid,* and the *Ballad of Harry Bridges.* "We walked down the aisle on our way out and they slapped Woody on the back so hard they nearly knocked him over."

> There once was a Union Maid,
> She never was afraid
> Of goons and ginks and company finks
> And the deputy sheriffs that made the raid.
> She went to the Union hall
> When a meeting it was called,
> And when the comp'ny boys came 'round she always
>   stood her ground.
>
> *Chorus*
> Oh, you can't scare me, I'm sticking to the Union,

I'm sticking to the Union,
I'm sticking to the Union.
Oh, you can't scare me, I'm sticking to the Union,
I'm sticking to the Union—till the day I die.

Back in New York in the fall of 1941, the Almanac Singers moved into a narrow three-story building on West 10th Street and called it Almanac House. It was freezing cold that winter. In spite of the many bookings at unions and "cause" parties, there was seldom enough to pay the rent and feed the six or seven regulars, plus any others who might drop in for a meal or an overnight stay. Sometimes complete strangers sat down at the long table, ate, and then disappeared, never to be seen again. Lee Hays, the chief cook and baker of fresh, fragrant bread, managed to feed them all.

Almanac House was a busy place, with people coming and going, with projects and ideas always up for discussion. Many came with their instruments to pick up pointers from Pete and Woody.

House expenses were covered by the Sunday afternoon Hootenannies, a word Pete and Woody had picked up in the Pacific Northwest. It was originally a rural word for a thing-a-ma-jig. An Almanac Hootenanny meant a grab bag of songs by the group, singing by the audience, and yarn spinning by anyone who cared to. New talent was always welcome. For the price of thirty-five cents, visitors could come and stay as long as they liked. And so they did— bringing their own pillows, or sitting on mattresses or on coats spread flat on the floor.

Those were marvelous afternoons. Leadbelly and his wife Martha came by, and Earl Robinson brought his boy Perry. And there was Woody, singing with his head thrown back, his black hair looking like a thick mat.

Nevertheless, hard times and the cold winter of 1941–42 had its effect on the Almanacs. There was never enough money to keep a whole building warm and often the only source of heat came from the kitchen gas oven turned up full force. As for those foolish enough to spend the night in the upper floors of the House—well, all through the night you could hear their teeth chattering! When money for coal gave out, the Almanacs and their friends would go out scavenging the neighborhood for burnable items—old discarded furniture and broken orange crates. At the last Hootenanny held in the house, heat was provided by burning back copies of *The New York Times*. Woody wrote a blues about the icy conditions of Almanac House, one verse of which went,

> I went into the bathroom and I pulled the chain,
> Polar bears on icebergs came floating down the drain,
> Hey, pretty mama, I got those Arctic Circle blues.

Woody had only one set of clothes left: a red plaid flannel shirt (faded and worn in spots), a wrinkled pair of pants, a thin jacket, a pair of old worn-out shoes, and an old army overcoat that was at least two or three sizes too big for him. Often he worked through the night, occasionally filling his cup with coffee made from twice-used grounds, clacking away at his typewriter until he fell asleep, utterly exhausted, in front of the stove.

By midwinter the Almanacs were served notice of eviction for nonpayment of rent. They found a new place on Sixth Avenue near 9th Street, and rounded up volunteers to do the moving, since there was no money to hire regular movers. Because many of the volunteers had jobs during the day, the moving was done on foot after midnight. Gordon Freisen, then with the Almanacs, wrote,

> It was like ants moving from an old colony to a new one. In one direction proceeded a file of Almanacs and supporters, lamp shades on their heads, boxes of books and papers or articles of furniture in their arms; some carried

113

beds (the old-fashioned kind with casters) piled high with clothes, bedding, etc. As this line pressed more or less steadily forward it was passed by a silent file of empty-handed ants returning to Almanac House for fresh loads.

Woody, then in the midst of writing a book, paid no attention to the hubbub around him. He kept typing away while furniture, bedding, pots and pans were being removed. The house grew colder and colder, for the front door was left open to facilitate the moving. By sun-up the operation was over. The last things to go were the typewriter and the kitchen table on which it rested. Later that day some of the Almanacs came back for a last search. They found Woody sound asleep, curled up on the cold linoleum floor in front of the open oven, which still radiated a little warmth. They left him there, hunched up tight as a ball "under a spread out copy of the *N. Y. Journal-American,* his manuscript beside him." A few days later he turned up at the new Sixth Avenue Almanac House, staked out a corner for himself and his typewriter, and went back to work on his book as if nothing had happened.

That winter Woody met Marjorie Mazia, a dancer, whom he later married and who was to become the mother of four children: Cathy, Arlo, Joady, and Nora.

Since Marjorie Guthrie was and is the true chronicler of Woody's life at this time, it would be most appropriate to let her tell the story of their early days:

◆   While I was on tour with Martha Graham's Dance Group in 1941, I visited my sister in Columbia, Missouri. When I arrived, she said, "Marge, I've got a great record to play for you," and she played *Tom Joad,* sung and written by someone called Woody Guthrie. Tears poured down my cheeks. I can remember gripping the seat and being terribly moved.

Several months later back in New York, Sophie Maslow, also in Martha Graham's company, said to me, "I want to do a couple of dances to folk music.   Woody Guthrie's in town and I'm going to ask him to do the music."

"Good God," I said, "I've got to meet that man!"   In my mind I pictured a Lincolnesque figure, tall, thin, scrawny looking and wearing a cowboy hat.   That was the image I had gotten from his voice.

Sophie and I went down to the Sixth Avenue Almanac House where he was living.   We knocked and a big, fat man answered the door.   It was Arthur Stern, a member of the group.   He wouldn't let us in.   "Woody is sleeping," he said, "come back some other time."

"We've brought him some fruit," we said ingratiatingly, and tried to push past him.

He barred the door.   "Why don't you leave it?" he asked.

"We don't want to leave it," we told him, "we want to give it to him personally."

After much persuasion he let us in.   There were several large, circular columns in the Almanac House, and in between them, with his back to us, was this little, scrawny figure facing the windows.

Sophie called out, "Woody?"   He turned around and looked at me.   I knew right then and there that I was going to marry him.   I didn't know when, but I was sure about it!

"Woody," we said, "we've brought you some fruit."   Shyly he walked over to us.   After all, he didn't know either of us.

Sophie explained the project she had in mind, a dance based on a few of his Dust Bowl songs, which he would sing and she would dance.   He seemed to like the idea although he didn't say much.   Eventually Sophie choreographed not only the two songs, but also a group dance called "Folksay" based in part on Carl Sandburg's *We, The People*.   Woody sang and acted the part of a country rube simpleton (who was really smart) and Earl Robinson, the composer, played the smart city slicker (who was really

115

dumb). Woody wrote a story called *Folksay* about our first work together, talking about himself and his first experience as an actor. It was his first experience at introspective writing and he sought anonymity behind the pseudonym of Tom Harris:

"Tom Harris was new to the whole thing, and the whole thing was new to him. Tom was too little to suit his own self but there never was much he could do about his body because he was a little hump-shouldered, dark bushy hair, bony and skinny. . . . He felt like he was ugly. So he sort of tried to put his ugly looks to good use. He was trying to be an actor . . . he could usually say all he had to say on the subject of acting in about a half-dozen words and from there on he mostly had to just listen. Tom had figured out that if you could always just simply be your own natural self in front of an audience and that if you knew enough about the ways of the world, well if you really had something to say, the people would like you and would listen."

Woody was a real story teller and could repeat a story over and over and always make us laugh. But after a few rehearsals, things began to go wrong. The dancers were annoyed because he never sang the song the same way twice. Sophie pleaded with me to do something or the dance would be ruined. It was one thing to sing a folk song and another to do it as a dance where everyone had to come in together. I finally figured out a way of counting the beats of the song and the beats between each line. All Woody had to do was memorize the numbers just as he memorized the words. I typed out the words in big capital letters and pasted them on shirt cardboards, like a book. The system worked beautifully.

We rehearsed for several months. It was not long before I realized that Woody was interested in me. We were clear about our feelings towards each other from the

116

very beginning but nothing was said or done for a while. I remember we had a party after the first performance of *Folksay* and we walked back to my room on West 14th Street. We went through the streets hand in hand, his finger touching mine through my torn glove. We spent that first night together—not making love—but talking to each other about his life and mine.

The first time Woody and I had a date, he appeared at my room on 14th Street in a formal suit, much too big for him. I had never seen him dressed in anything but pants and a plaid shirt before and it struck me so funny that I laughed until the tears ran down my face. And then we laughed together until our sides hurt. I never saw him in pants and jacket again.

The seriousness of our relationship was immediately apparent. I was married at that time and there were many problems to be solved before we could become man and wife.

Shortly after we met, Woody gave me a present, Leadbelly's record *Work Songs of the U.S.A.* (released by Moe Asch on the Folkways label). In it, he wrote this
♦ beautiful inscription:

"Dear Marjorie:
■ As I went walking down Sixth Avenue looking for a present to buy for a surprise, I looked in at about ten dozen jewelry shop windows and thought: she wouldn't like those bunch of grapes or that silver horse or that hand-beaten flower because her first husband is a metal worker and does all of that for her with the possible exception of the hand-beating, and this window full of innocent perfume, she had a lover in Alaska who soaked roses in alcohol, . . . I found windows reeling past and my head whirling faster, and not being anxious to even part with my money in the first place, I found myself almost backing out of the whole idea of a gift. And then

117

I decided I had to get tough.   The gift I buy had to be better than perfume and stronger than metal.   It had to be . . . the honesty of a saloon and the frenzy of a church. . . . So, when I heard Leadbelly's voice on these records, I thought: Here's the surprise I've been looking for!   SUR-
■ PRISE!—Woody   July 28, 1942, New York Town."

In December, 1941, America had gone to war.   National production went into an upswing and the national economy began to boom.   Woody found himself busy with bookings and auditions on top of his song writing.

The songs still came first, however, though they were now reflecting the atmosphere of wartime.   Essentially, Woody was a man of peace, but his hatred of the Nazis and their allies led him to take an active role in the war effort, both through his song writing and later through service in Europe with the U.S. Merchant Marine.

When the American warship *Reuben James* was torpedoed in the early months of the war with Germany, Woody and the Almanacs echoed the thoughts of all those who were losing friends and sons in the service:

It was there in the dark of that uncertain night,
That we watched for the U-boat and waited for a fight;
Then a whine and a rock and a great explosion roar,
And they laid the Reuben James on the cold ocean floor.

Tell me what were their names?
Tell me what were their names?
Did you have a friend on the good Reuben James?

The following year, three of the Almanacs—Woody, Pete, and Sis Cunningham—appeared at the Waldorf-Astoria Hotel before a convention of business executives.   By the time the group got up to sing it was late and the four or five hundred people in the hall were noisily drunk.   They opened with

118

several anti-fascist songs but could hardly be heard above the din. The audience wanted to be entertained, not instructed. Pete exploded with angry words, but no one was listening. A drunk sitting at one of the front tables bawled at them: "Aw, shut up, and play some music: *She'll Be Coming Round The Mountain.*" Woody took the next verse alone and sang loud and clear over the microphone:

She'll be wearin' a union button when she comes,
She'll be wearin' a union button when she comes,
She'll be wearin' a union button
She'll be wearin' a union button
She'll be wearin' a union button when she comes!

There was a full moment of silence when he finished. The singers packed their instruments and walked off the stage.

Another moment of silence, and again the cry arose, almost to a frenzy: "Bring on the girls! Bring 'em on!"

Woody resisted many attempts to remold him into a respectable citizen. He felt uncomfortable with the salesmen of Hollywood and Broadway, "the wheelers and the dealers, the fast talkers, the sex-excited men and women, the hypocrites." He kept out of their way as much as he could, even at the cost of earning the money he so urgently needed.

About the time the Almanac Singers broke up, an agent for the William Morris Agency, one of the largest theatrical agencies in New York, took an interest in Woody and the group. Woody's war songs (composed in collaboration with the Almanacs), *Round and Round Hitler's Grave* and *The Reuben James* were becoming popular, largely through the efforts of writer Norman Corwin. There was talk of a national tour, a network program of topical songs to be written on events of the day, and a contract with a leading record company. The agent arranged an audition at the Rainbow Room at Rockefeller Center.

Woody began:

This Rainbow Room she's mighty fine
You can spit from here to the Texas line!
In New York City
Lord, New York City
This is New York City, an I really gotta know my line.
This Rainbow Room is up so high
That John D's spirit comes a-driftin' by.

Pete Seeger reports the following lines:

> At the Rainbow Room the soup's on to boil,
> They're stirring the salad with Standard Oil.
> The Rainbow Room it's mighty high,
> You can see John D. a-flyin' by.

The management was worried about whether such songs would go over with their customers but figured that with the proper costumes—sunbonnets and gunny-sack dresses for the women and one-strap overalls for the men—and lights, and "hillbilly" clowning now and then, the act would make a hit. It never came off. Woody and the Almanac Singers walked out of the Rainbow Room never to return, partly because of their own negative feelings about the place and partly because a few days later they were red-baited in a New York newspaper. "Life is tough," Woody once said, "and you're lucky if you live through it."

The incident, however, strengthened his conviction that he was not a slick city entertainer and never was going to be one. "This is not for me, dressing up like a hillbilly and singing." He never changed his mind on that score: he was always a man of integrity, subservient to no one, the captive of nobody.

Woody and Marjorie were together all the time. One day, Marjorie said to him:

◆ "You don't really know what it's like to be a 'daily

worker' [the name of the newspaper of the Communist Party]. A daily worker is one who works from eight or nine in the morning to five or six in the evening. Then he does other things in the evening. Here you are writing about workers but you don't live like them."

"I like that," he said, "and I'm going to do it." And he did just that. It was hard for him to sit at his desk and write consistently but he saw the logic of it. Actually Woody wrote twenty-four hours a day in his heart. He was a writer, a born writer. It was just a question of
♦ discipline, and this he acquired as the years went by.

He was always noting things down, capturing events and his feelings about them, as if to fix them forever in time and space. Now Woody turned his attention to longer and more ambitious writings, including *Boomchasers,* the story of his early years. Alan Lomax arranged for the submission of the manuscript to the publishing firm of E. P. Dutton, and work began on Woody's first full-length book. Marjorie still remembers sitting up nights, taking turns with Woody at the typewriter as they typed up drafts for Woody to take down to his editor, Joy Doerflinger, the next day. The result was the autobiography, *Bound for Glory,* which still remains a classic of its kind.

It was some time before Marjorie received the divorce that enabled her to marry Woody. In the meantime, she was traveling back and forth from Philadelphia to New York, teaching in both places. While she was away, Cisco Houston was always there, comforting Woody, singing all night long with him, taking the edge off the lonely days and nights. At that time Cisco was living in New York, according to Woody, in ". . . an antique place. . . . The dresser goes back to Louis 14th, the table back to Henry 8th and his radio back to Gimbel's." *

Woody and Cisco walked the streets of Manhattan, on Ninth

* A large department store in New York City.

Avenue, near the docks and the Staten Island ferry, and sang for children playing in the streets and women sitting at their tenement windows. "Thank the lord," he wrote, "everybody is not all slicked up, and starched and imitation." Leaving the studios of WNYC, he would walk like a Pied Piper, with a crowd behind him, down Park Row near Brooklyn Bridge, into Chinatown.

One night Woody and his California friend Mike Quinn performed at an Unemployed Council meeting. They collected the agreed fee of seventy-five cents, which bought them a bottle of wine and left a nickel each for subway fare. They started singing for the passengers, with Woody playing the guitar. As the train swung downtown they picked up another singer and rode back and forth from Brooklyn to the Bronx singing one song after another. They ended up with a pocket full of coins and were proud to have earned it in this way—pennies, nickels and dimes from a lot of people, many of whom could probably hardly spare it!

When Marjorie became pregnant, they moved to an apartment on Charles Street in Greenwich Village which Woody called "Our Rancho Del Sol," or "Our Sun Ranch." He was sure that the baby was going to be a boy (it was a girl) and they invented fabulous stories about this child they called Pete. They also planned to call a second child "Repete." After Cathy Ann was born he wrote a book called *Stackabones,* his special name for her. As yet unpublished, this memoire reflects the warmth of Woody's family life.

■ Did you know that we both joked about how you was going to be a boy baby? Or did your mama tell you this yet? Yes sir.

Both of us always talked about you coming out to be a big ruffy tuffy boy with a tuff cap and a tightneck sweater, and a loud guitar, and a spittoon, and we already called you by the nickname of Railroad Pete. Railroad Pete. Union Man. Union Worker. Union Singer, Un-

■ ion Fighter, and a Nazi-Buster, and a Fascist-Cracker.

122

Cathy was born in Philadelphia and Woody came to see her in the hospital.

> I run up real close in behind you and the nurse and I asked
> her, hey, lady, say, lady,
>> can I take just one little free peek up in
>> under that bundle and that blanket you're
>> carrying there?
> And she said back acrost her shoulder to me running,
>> Nope siree sir.   You can not do that for sure.   You
>> have germs on you.
> And I told her
>> I've not got a single germ on me
>> If you don't believe me
>> Well, you can search me.

from *Stackabones*

When Marjorie brought Cathy back to Brooklyn she and Woody moved into a little room just above her father and mother's apartment in "an old dry, firetrap house," as Woody called it, in Sea Gate.   Then they moved a few blocks away, just outside the Sea Gate fence, over into Coney Island, into a brick building.   They had a bright three-room apartment there, and Woody loved it.   That was where they lived when the other three children—Arlo, Joady and Nora—were born.

During Marjorie's first pregnancy, Woody shipped out in the Merchant Marine with his guitar, "and two seaman buddies, . . . both good National Maritime Union (NMU) men: Cisco Houston, a guitar player and high tenor singer, and Jimmy Longhi, an Italian boy with as good an anti-fascist head on him as I have ever seen."   Woody continued to make music, even on the high seas of a war-torn world.

■   We played our guitars and I took along a fiddle and a mandolin.   Our first boat was torpedoed off the coast of Sicily, pulled into Lake Bizerte, but we got to visit the old bombed town of four hundred thousand souls, Palermo, Sicily, where Jimmy walked us up a mountainside singing underground songs to prisoners of war, and the people laughed and cried and shook our hands.

We caught an empty Liberty ship back to the States, and sailed out again to North Africa. We walked around to several of the most pitiful Arab villages that I have ever seen. We saw whole swarms of people race out of their rock and mud huts to fight like cats and dogs over a hunk of soap, and then to run away again when the soap was torn into a hundred pieces. We heard these people pound on their native skin drums and sing some of the saddest and prettiest music
■ that I have ever heard anywhere.

When he returned from North Africa Woody recorded an enormous collection of songs. In the introduction to a later book, *American Folksong,* he wrote:

■ Back in the States after this trip, Cisco Houston, Blind Sonny Terry and myself went up to the Asch studios. Moe Asch, son of Sholem Asch, took us in, cranked up his machinery and told us to fire away with everything that we had. We yelled and whooped and beat and pounded till Asch had taken down One Hundred and Twenty Some Odd Master sides. We tried hilltop and sunny mountain harmonies and wilder yells and whoops of the dead sea deserts, and all of the swampy southland and buggy bottom sounds that we could make. We sung to the mossy trees and to the standing moon, and Moe Asch and Marian Distler [Asch's assistant] worked through their
■ plate glass there in the recording studio.

His respect and admiration were boundless for the black artist, Sonny Terry:

■ Sonny Terry blew and whipped, beat, fanned, and petted

124

his harmonica, cooed to it like a weed hill turtle dove, cried to it like some worried woman come to ease his worried mind. He blew it down two to one and let it down easy, flipped his lip over and across and his tongue sending all of his wind into one hole, straining the reed with too much pressure and making it sound like it had several side tones and tones that dance between. He put the tobacco sheds of North and South Carolina in it and all of the blistered and hurt and hardened hands cheated and left empty, hurt and left crying, robbed and left hungry, pilfered and left starving, beaten and left dreaming. He rolled down the trains that the colored hand cannot drive, only clean and wash down. He blew into the wood holes and the brassy reeds the tale and the wails of Lost John running away from the dogs of the chain gang guards, and the chain gang
■ is the landlord that is never around anywhere.

Again Woody, Cisco, and Jim Longhi shipped out and were torpedoed off the coast of Normandy. They spent three weeks in Britain and then returned to the States on May 8, 1945, the day the war ended in Europe. Woody was soon drafted into the army and remained in barracks until Japan surrendered in September.

While he was a civilian, Woody, according to Marjorie Guthrie, lived pretty much as he wanted and made up his own rules.

♦   In the Merchant Marines the men gave him a lot of leeway. It was his job to set the tables every day. Not Woody! He was too busy writing the news on his blackboard, or inventing fancy menus. He did the extras but didn't set up the table. The guys never got sore. They let him decorate his bulletin board without interfering.

The army was another story. Woody was stationed at Scott Field, Illinois, where, besides drilling, wearing a uniform, and getting up at bugle call, he did cleanup duty.

125

Woody went to work with a vengeance. To his mind, cleanliness in an army camp and beating the Nazis were the same thing. Apparently the others didn't think so. Two guys walked over to him.

"What are you doing?" they asked.

"Making Scott Field clean, what you think?"

They made it very clear to him to slow down. For them it was going to be a three-day job, not one day. Woody was horrified. He wrote to me saying, "What kind of a war effort is this to do a job in three days when it could be done in one day!" He was that way about everything that had to do with the war. During this time I received a mountain of correspondence, and, of course, he wrote many, many songs. Here are a few verses from
◆ *Turkey In The Corn,* which he wrote in Scott Field.

In a little bed a woman was born
In a little house a man was born
In a little time my baby was born
To run like a turkey in my green June corn.

River come up and took my boards
Vine come up and give me the gourds
Baby learned words from the winds and storms
To run like a turkey through my green June corn.

My kitten it growed and my dog got bred
Old blind mare she fell down dead
Another little baby was born in my arm
To run like a turkey in my green June corn.

"(This come to me in the Army Camp at Scott Field, Ill., one hot summers day looking over the fence at a big patch of green corn.)"

"(Sometimes I think I ain't nothing but an old piece of dirt walking.)"

126

With the war's end in 1945, Woody returned to his usual routine. Woody's friend, folksinger Hally Wood, recalls him in postwar New York:

In the years after World War II you might have met Woody wandering around New York, in a pea jacket handed down from Marjorie's brother, with his guitar on his back—the one marked "this machine kills fascists." He was little known, thoroughly unprepossessing, an oddity on Times Square but quite unselfconscious, at home anywhere. He was small and delicately built, with fine hands and feet and hairless arms, though there was nothing effeminate about him. His features were regular and somewhat sharp. His smile was angelic, erasing all the tension around his eyes so that he looked at happy moments like a child.

Like the rest of the folk singers in New York, Woody couldn't have fed himself on what singing brought in. Some had regular jobs and sang on the side. People's Songs was organized to provide us with a way of earning some money. There were many parties in those days for hand-picked lists of guests from the entertainment, radio, and recording industry, in the hope that they would find jobs for us. We met people like Lena Horne and Joe Louis.

Alan Lomax worked hardest at planning concerts and selling folk music to record companies. Most of us owe him more than we can ever repay. And if it hadn't been for Moe Asch, Woody would have been even poorer than he was. Altogether it was slim pickings until the Weavers made a hit with *So Long, It's Been Good to Know You.*

Marjorie saw another, personal, unpleasant byproduct of the parties: Unable to go because of her own working schedule, she would sit up waiting, only to be called the next morning by an embarrassed husband who hadn't come home that night.

"I guess I was jealous. . . . In the years before he really be-

127

came famous many women fell in love with him. They were interesting people, motherly women, who wanted to take care of him. He always looked helpless. . . ."

But family life survived somehow:

♦   After we had Cathy our house in Coney Island was open to every child on the block.

Many of the families were too poor and their houses too crowded to have living rooms. The teenagers took over empty stores and fixed them up with old couches and broken-down furniture. Their windows opened into our backyard and we would hear them playing pop music all hours of the night. Woody would always say, if they could only hear his music. Little by little we became friends with these kids; they were our baby sitters and they played chess with Woody. Later on when Cathy was dying in the hospital and needed blood, the boys from the club helped out.

We lived in a small-town atmosphere. The people in Coney Island were good to us. Woody's clothes didn't matter. His long beard, if he wanted to grow one, didn't matter. They were receptive to nice people, and we were nice people.

Woody liked them too. His affection for them wasn't superficial, it was real. Everybody loved watching him write and do his art work. He always had a feeling for the arts, even as a child.

When we lived in Brooklyn he used to spend weeks working on collages which he called Hoodis. He made them out of odd things I had in the house—pennies, stones, and pieces of rubber balls, bits of glass, and shells. My mother brought him her collection of old pieces of jewelry for the Hoodis. To Woody there was no such thing as junk. My favorite was one I called *Oneness*—half a yoyo set on a piece of rock. Woody added a lot of little things and it looked like a sea creature opened up with things dripping out of it. He loved entertaining the children with his

+ Hoodis. Woody wrote:

"To me, a hoodis goes to show you that you can take all of your ugliest things, your brokest and your worn outtest things, and stick them together the ways mama nature does her leaves and her stems and her weeds and her grass-blades, and make out of your trashiest things your very nicest and prettiest of flowers."

+ He made pictures for the children, and labeled everything the children made. I still have things that Arlo made as a young child with Woody's funny explanations written on
+ them.

———— ◆·— ————

The postwar years were particularly productive despite poverty and personal tragedy. In February of 1947, when she was four years old, the adored, beloved Miss Stackabones was fatally burned in an accident caused by faulty wiring. She sang her little songs even in the hospital, until the last breath in her body was gone. Woody was perhaps haunted by memories of Clara, but he and Marjorie went on working; it was their only salvation. Two days after Cathy's death they performed together, Woody singing while Marjorie led children in dancing.

Fortunately, Marjorie, who was pregnant again, was able to weather this terrible time. Arlo Davy Guthrie was born in July. A year and a half later Joady Ben was born, and in the winter of 1950, Nora Lee. Once more the Guthrie household was filled with laughter, games, and music. The children made drums of oatmeal boxes, decorated ash cans and banged on them, and played on tuned glasses. Woody rattled his spoons, sang his songs, and wrote lullabies for his children:

Goodnight, Little Arlo, Goodnight!
Goodnight, Little Arlo, Goodnight!
Sleep, sleep, sleepy, sleep tight, sleep tight!
Goodnight, Little Arlo,
Goodnight!

You've played, little Ziberzee all day;
With dollies and wagons and clay.
Your bath it's warm and your 'jammers are tight!
Goodnight, Little Arlo, Goodnight.

Although Woody was writing prodigiously at home while Marjorie taught in the city, the Guthries were often found on the beach at Coney Island, the first to arrive and the last to leave.

Woody spent a lot of time with the children.   Arlo was closest, never letting his father out of his sight.

Woody's powers of concentration were extraordinary, for he was able to work at his desk and keep his eye on the children at the same time.   He was a methodical worker and capable of writing as many as five songs a day.   Every day he would start in on a cycle of songs based on "the muse of the day" and he would always follow the same routine:

1—write the song down
2—try it out on the guitar
3—revise the song, and then
4—write down three more titles and start in on them.

Woody was not only writing and performing frequently (for slim fees) all over the country, but studying as well.   In 1950 he enrolled at Brooklyn College, taking courses in English, Philosophy, and Classical Civilization.   It was a wonderful experience, for he had always wanted to go to college.   His English teacher commented that Woody's writing was the finest she had ever received from a student.   Marjorie often wondered what direction his work would have taken if he had had the time.

Woody was just beginning to understand aspects of the arts he had never known about. He saw dances by Martha Graham and her company (Marjorie was still a member), attended plays, listened to classical music, and once again visited the library regularly.

Marjorie still remembers the armloads of books that Woody would bring home. He read on every conceivable subject, though his manner of doing so was rather unorthodox: Woody was capable of reading 5 or 6 books at once, turning his attention to each book for perhaps an hour at a time before going on to the next one. As a result, there were always 5 or 6 books, each open to a specific page, lying around the house at every conceivable eye level and on every conceivable article of furniture. Each volume seemed to be bearing an invisible sign saying **DO NOT DISTURB.** And the family obeyed.

Woody was impressed by the discipline exacted by the art forms he saw. "He was accustomed to singing only when he felt like it," his wife said.

◆　He and Cisco could sing a song like *Poor Howard* all day long. I'd leave them in the morning singing

> "Poor old Howard's dead and gone,
> Left me here to sing this song.
> Pretty little girl with the red dress on."

and come back in the evening to find them still singing it. And here I was running to rehearsals whether I felt like it or not, because it was my job. He would come with me to the studio to watch the dancers arriving on time, no matter what the weather, practicing even when they were sick. It made a terrific impact on him.

I don't want you to think our life was a bed of roses. We had very violent arguments. Woody left me many times, but always came back. I was as stubborn as he was, and very vocal. He would say a few mean words and I would

131

fly off the handle: "Get out!"   He'd pick up his guitar, sling it on his back, and walk.   He'd disappear for three or four days.   I'd cry the whole time.   Then he'd be at the door again.

We fought about important things—children, home, and a good deal about money; sometimes about drinking and he'd yell, "I've been drinking since I was four years old!   I drank wine like it was water.   You come from a different kind of background and that's why you feel this way!"

He was happiest when he was working.   The last book he wrote, *Silver Mine,* took eight months.   During that time he hardly drank at all, and when he did it made him
◆ violently ill.

Nineteen fifty-one was a turning point in Woody's life.   The Weavers' recording of *So Long, It's Been Good to Know You* made the Hit Parade and rocketed him to fame.   Woody received a check for $1200 and cashed it into small bills.

"I remember him coming home with the money," says Marjorie, "and throwing it all over the place.   It wasn't enough to say, 'Here's twelve hundred dollars.'   It had to be thrown, it had to be blown.   I was still finding dollar bills behind the furniture for weeks afterward!"

That was only the beginning.   Suddenly, doors began swinging open everywhere.   There were offers of contracts and royalties on songs suddenly jumped.   Now, at 39, he was to be free at last of the poverty that had plagued him all his life.   Now he could assume the burden of earning a living for his wife and children.

But it was too late: the illness that was to carry Woody off sixteen years later had already begun on its destructive path, bringing him slowly but inevitably to the end of the road.

132

Coney Island, New York, 1946: Cathy Guthrie, "Miss Stackabones."

July, 1947: Woody and the "Hoodis."

Woody Guthrie, 1948.

Marjorie Mazia Guthrie, 1948.

About 1949: Ice cream break at Marjorie Guthrie "dance party" in Newark, New Jersey. L. to r.: Jack Elliott, Woody, unidentified adult dance student.

Summer in Coney Island, 1949, l. to r.:
Joady, Woody, Arlo, Marjorie.

September, 1950, l. to r.: top—Doll,
Arlo, Joady, Woody, Nora. Bottom—
Doll, Arlo, Joady, Marjorie, Nora.

Coney Island, August, 1951, l. to r.:
Nora, Joady, Woody, Arlo.

Early 1950s, at a party for Woody, standing l. to r.: Arlo, Will Geer, Cisco Houston, Lee Hays, Mill Lampell; seated: Woody, Nora, Sonny Terry.

Woody's last picture, 1966, with Harold Leventhal, Arlo, and Marjorie.

LAST YEARS

M ARJORIE GUTHRIE CAN BEST DESCRIBE the events of those final years. What should have been a period of consolidation and reward turned into a time of progressive decline.

♦ What confused me, and Woody himself, in the early stage of the illness, was that by nature he was a rather moody person. As early as 1948, we began to notice that he was more reflective, and often depressed by trivial things.

Woody decided that it would be better for him to work away from home. He rented a store around the corner and we helped him cart books and typewriter, in Cathy's four-wheeler wagon. We bought a hot plate so he could make coffee, and made shelves out of orange crates. Woody stayed only a few days and then gradually moved his belongings back to the house. We rented five such

♦ places, with the same frustrating result.

Such were the beginnings of Woody's illness, as observed by his family. Woody himself was very distressed:

■ . . . I was absolutely so unable to work [at home] that, well, I had to walk around there and rent me some little

workroom, cellars you know, to do my workings in; and
each little workingroom turned out to be more of a flop-
house where I stumbled and fell down amongst my songs
and papers dogdrunk deaddrunk and so messed up in general that—well, I got some few things done, I guess but not
one-sixteenth thing of what I had cravened to get done; so I
got to feeling so much like a guilty failure that I felt worse
than some kind of a raper or a killer or a raving madman.
. . . I was afraid to look any earthly human in the face,
■ and more afraid to look them in the eye.

Finally the Guthries moved to a more expensive apartment
in Beach Haven.   A young runaway (and future folk singer)
named Jack Elliott wandered in and stayed, helping with the
children and becoming Woody's close companion.   He was
one of many young people who found their way to the Guthrie door, knocked, and asked, "Where's Woody?"   In later
years their numbers included a couple of kids named Phil
Ochs and Bob Dylan; the Guthries always had room for them.
By this time the symptoms of the disease had become more
obvious.   Woody developed a peculiar lopsided walk and his
speech became explosive.   He would take a deep sigh before
breathing out the words.   The moods and depressions became more exaggerated and more frequent.
Time was running out and Woody sensed it:

■   I don't choose nor want to make any more sadder mis-
takes than I've already made around this map of ours. . . .
I'm not the great, great, hero of the masses that many
minds have drempt me to be; but I'm sure not the rubbout,
deadlygone failure that many others say I have been.   I
am somewhere just in between all of this and these guesses,
hunches, and opinions.   I know the full value of the gifts
and talents I can make to the labor movement . . . but I
am quick to admit and to know that I've got to play now
for keeps and for fast, and to go for broke; I have to pro-

tect my works now because they are at longlast turning into things that (like any factory job) make money; and I don't choose if I can steer clear of it to chase out on wild drunken sprees and loud verbal sprees and to waste away all these things I've been mudbuilding now for such long sea-
■ sons of times and tides.

Despite his condition he continued to make plans for the future: a new singing group, not polished like the Weavers, but acceptable to city audiences. The dream was never realized.

Marjorie never forgot the first attack:

◆ One night in 1952 Woody had a violent outburst and foamed at the mouth. Something was going wrong and we were alarmed. At six o'clock that morning I called Earl Robinson, and he drove us to Brooklyn State Hospital. It was barely light when we got there.

Despite his physical ailment he was the same old fighting Woody. On entering, he was asked his religion.

"All," replied Woody firmly.

"Mr. Guthrie, we must know which religion to list you as."

"All."

"I'm sorry, Mr. Guthrie, it must be one or another."

"All or none," said Woody.

Woody stayed in the hospital for three weeks.

"They think I'm an alcoholic," he said, when I came to visit him, "maybe it's alcoholic depression." When he came home, he took out every book on alcoholism from the library. Then we called the A.A. (Alcoholics Anonymous) and they sent two very nice guys to visit him. Really, it was funny! They simply did not understand him, although he understood them all too well. We agreed that the A.A. was not for him.

About a week later, he took a room on West 14th Street in the same building where I had lived when we first

141

met. He didn't want the children to see him in another attack. A few nights later I had a call from him—another violent seizure. I knew that he was completely distraught. I rushed to him as fast as I could and took him to Bellevue Hospital, a short distance away.

He stayed there for three months. For a few weeks everything went well; he had made friends with everyone in the ward and they all loved him. But then more attacks came and Woody was confined to a locked ward as a precaution for himself and others.

One day the telephone rang; Woody was calling from the hospital. For a moment I thought he had escaped.

"I'm downstairs," he said, "and the doctor told me to go home."

"Do you have money for the subway?" I asked.

"Yes."

"Then come home!"

Meanwhile, I called the doctor at Bellevue.

"Is it possible," I said, "that you have released my husband without a diagnosis, without even letting me know?" I have not forgotten his exact words: "Mrs. Guthrie, your husband is a very sick man, and we don't know what to do with him."

Woody stayed home a short while. He would lie on the bed for days, hardly saying a word to anyone. Even the children hesitated before speaking to him. He was steadily getting worse. A solution had to be found. He would go to California. California was warm and he had friends there, he could stay with Will Geer, who was then on the West

♦ Coast.

In actuality, this California trip was the beginning of the end. Woody went back and forth across the country during the next few years. By this time he and Marjorie had agreed to part: they both knew that he faced years in the hospital, that the costs would be astronomical, and that Marjorie, as his

142

wife, would be liable for them. Perplexed, they turned to a lawyer friend, who advised them in all seriousness to get a divorce. At the time, they regarded it as a purely legal step that would free Marjorie—who had three children to support—of an intolerable financial burden. But as the divorce papers were drawn up, they mused on the irony of the situation.

For a while Woody traveled with Jack Elliott, who sang, as Woody put it, more like him than he did himself. Together they made their way toward California and the new folk song center at Topango Canyon, north of Santa Monica. There, at Will Geer's house, Woody met a young girl he called Annie, who returned to New York with him. The divorce from Marjorie went through, and Annie became Woody's wife. It was a brief, unhappy marriage; Woody's young friend had not realized the extent of his illness and was ill-equipped to care for a sick man.

By now the disease was making rapid strides. Woody found it increasingly difficult to control his movements, appearing to be drunk even when he wasn't drinking. Friends watched with apprehension as he dived into traffic oblivious of danger, Chaplin-like, warding off each car as it sped toward him. Sometimes he hung around the office of the Stinson Recording Company, a pioneer producer of folk music in downtown New York, listening to young people as they sang his songs. Occasionally he would appear, bearded and long-haired, playing a mandolin to Jack Elliott's guitar at the fountain in Washington Square Park, the mecca for young folk singers in New York.

On the surface it appeared that Woody was floating and drifting through life in those years. Still the idol of politically oriented audiences, he was making contact with the younger people who were to become the "Beat Generation." Writers like Jack Kerouac and poet Allan Ginsberg knew of him. Kerouac, whose early writings resembled Woody's, rejected him arrogantly. In a conversation with John Cohen of The New Lost City Ramblers, he said, "Woody is just

143

a folk singer. I am a poet like Rimbaud and Verlaine."
On the other hand, Ginsberg liked Woody's spirit, honesty
and frankness.

Ironically, as Woody's illness deepened, he became the idol
of the younger generation, not as a folk hero, but for the way
he lived, for his frank language, his disregard for established
conventions. Even the physical characteristics of his disease
—the jerkiness and halting speech—were imitated by his
young followers. But in this case they misunderstood him:
their idol was sick and they copied the manifestations of his
illness.

Then one day Annie came to Marjorie for help. Woody's
condition had deteriorated to the point where she could no
longer take care of him at home. It was left to Marjorie to
take him back to Brooklyn State Hospital on what must have
been the blackest day of her life. From that time on, she remained by Woody's side until the very end. Some time later,
Annie obtained a divorce and returned to California.

Woody was brought back to the hospital for the last time,
running a temperature of 103 degrees.

"I'm here because I have to be here," he told Dr. Abe
Glenn, who had admitted him four years earlier. "I know it,
and I'm going to stay now."

Marjorie pressed Dr. Glenn, who had become a family
friend. "This has been going on for four years," she
cried. "Can't somebody tell us what's wrong with
Woody?" Dr. Glenn promised to find out. A few months
later, a young doctor came up with the truth—Woody had
Huntington's Disease. Marjorie remembers holding Woody's
hand as the doctor told them the news:

◆   "What do we do now?" I said.
    "Well," said Woody, "I stay here and you raise the chil-
dren."
    And that's the way it remained. It was 1956, and
Woody was only forty-four years old.

Woody's mother had died in an insane asylum. Years later we learned that she had actually died of Huntington's Disease. Medical books mistakenly claimed that the disease was transmitted only to the female. Now, of course, we know differently.

We learned to accept the situation. Woody and I told the children the truth because we felt that they could face anything if they knew what it was. The dark is always more
♦ frightening than the light of day.

> The Committee to Combat Huntington's Disease, set up in June, 1967, owes its existence primarily to Mrs. Marjorie Guthrie. It was organized to help support research into the causes, effects and treatment of the disease, to aid the victims and their families to cope with their various problems, and to help disseminate information to the general public.

♦ In the early years of his stay in hospitals, Woody would leave every now and then on his own. One day he took the wrong bus and landed in some town in New Jersey. Noticing his disheveled appearance, his distraught air and halting gait, a policeman picked him up, took him to the local police station, and booked him on a vagrancy charge.

Woody told the police that he was not a homeless bum but a sick man. He explained that he was staying at a New York hospital and begged them to get him home. "Well," they said, "if you're sick you can stay in our hospital." Finally, they let him call me and I went tearing out to New Jersey.

When I arrived I was received by a staff doctor, a Viennese psychiatrist. "Your husband is a very disturbed man," he said imperiously, "with many hallucinations. He says that he has written a thousand songs."

"It is true," I said.

"He also says he has written a book!"

145

"That's also true."

"He says that a record company has put out nine records of his songs!" The doctor's voice dripped disbelief.

♦   "That is also the truth," I said.

Woody remained there for three years. During that time, he was occasionally permitted outside for public appearances. John Cohen brought him to Alan Lomax' big program, *Folk Song 1959,* held at Carnegie Hall. Sitting for once in a loge, Woody recited the words of *Deportee,* his song about the death of Mexican workers in a plane accident, while Pete Seeger sang it on stage:

Goodbye to my Juan, goodbye, Rosalita,
Adios mis amigos, Jesus y Maria;
You won't have your names when you ride the big airplane,
All they will call you will be deportees.

My Father's own Father, he waded that river,
They took all the money he made in his life;
My brothers and sisters come working the fruit trees,
And they rode the truck till they took down and died.

Once in a while Woody appeared on Oscar Brand's folk song program over WNYC radio. But in general, it was a long and lonely period. Jack Elliott was in England. Friends who lived near the hospital sometimes took him home for a day or two. Bob Dylan was among those who visited him toward the end of his stay in New Jersey. Due to the red tape involved, his transfer to New York took a long time and he was very happy to come back. The rest is Marjorie's story:

♦   Sometimes he went out to sing with the crowd in Washington Square Park. Many young people used to gather around the fountain in the middle of the park to sing folk songs and play banjos and guitars—but it was too late for Woody; he found it too hard to tune his guitar, too hard to play.

In the summer of 1955, the children of Camp Hawthorne in Kaiser, Missouri, learned *This Land Is Your Land* and became interested in its creator. When they learned that Woody was in the hospital, they wrote him a letter to tell him how much they loved his songs. Here is his reply:

"I am Woody Guthrie and I'm forty-three years old and I sure never got a letter that makes me feel as fine and as good as yours does. . . . Keep more spinnin' in around me.

"I love warm-hearted, true, friendly letters made and painted by hand like yours better than any old high-printed picture card I ever got, so write me lots more to keep weller on. . . .

"I can very plainly tell you that your big brown envelope of good letters from Camp Hawthorne has helped me more than all my nurses and all my doctors all added up.

"I'm sure glad God made me sick enough to make you one and all my pretty angels and send me out such nice letters as yours are.

"Your letter has got me walkin' and a-talkin' up and down my roadway here tryin' to think up a song a little bit better than your pet, This Land."

Woody stayed in Brooklyn State Hospital from 1956 to 1965. When he received the award from the Department of the Interior he was moved to Creedmoor State Hospital, Long Island, and there he spent the remaining two years of his life.

He was determined to make a life for himself even in the hospital. He was always so positive, always joyous, always believing. In fact, he continued writing even though it was difficult. I have kept the many, many pages he

147

wrote during those years. He speaks of loving people—
"the dear doctors, my dear nurses, my dear fellow patients"
—that kind of thing!

Within a short time he knew the life story of every patient
in the ward. Everyone opened up to him; everyone loved
him. Then he would tell me about it. When I came with
cigarettes he would lead me around to the patients who had
none. I visited the people who had no family or
friends. He shared whatever he had with the others, and
that meant sharing visitors too.

Occasionally I took him home for the weekend. As
soon as he heard my voice from the other end of the hospital
corridor, he would come, shuffling with his poor gait, ready
to leave without his coat, even in the bitterest cold
weather. In later years when he could no longer manage
the stairs, a friend would come to help out. We'd carry him
down, one arm supporting his neck, the other around his
waist. He'd hang on to both of us, practically racing us
down the stairs.

Woody always loved the sun, he loved grass. This had
been part of his life, the outdoors, looking up at the
sky. When he came home weekends in the early part of his
confinement, he would lie on a cot out in the back yard,
half dressed, half undressed. He loved the sun to shine on
his body.

In Huntington's the body metabolism doesn't work
properly. Woody needed lots of food, and lots of
sweets. When he came home weekends we would feed him
tons of food. This was a big joke for the children: How
many frankfurters would he take that day? Six; and how
many milks? He'd take four. And how many cakes?
He'd take six. And how many root beers? And whatever.

The children saw him at close hand on these occasions
but never at the hospital. Young children are not allowed
there. I used to bring them to the lawn down below so he

could see them.   In the spring he would sit out on the terrace.   The children would dance and make faces at him, and he would yell and talk back to them.   I don't really know how the children felt about his illness; perhaps one day they will talk about it.

I kept alive all the great stories about Woody.   It was a way of keeping my family alive.   Arlo said that "Woody was in the house even when he was in the hospital.   And he's still hanging around.   Who can say where someone begins and ends?"

During those years there were many letters from old friends and others, young and old, who wanted to visit him in the hospital.   The truth is that I did not encourage them, particularly in the last years when Woody was in a wheelchair and unable to speak.   It upset him because he couldn't communicate.   Sometimes I would bring people with me because I felt that Woody would be happy just seeing the person—visually.   We would talk with each other about our children, about happenings in the world and Woody would just listen and enjoy the conversation.

Music was really the best way of communicating.   I particularly remember one day when his old friends—Pete Seeger, Sonny Terry, Brownie McGhee, and Cisco—came to Brooklyn State to play for him.   It was a joyous occasion; yes, it was!   Pete was upset when he first walked in so I said, "Woody, you must prove that you understand everything we're saying even though you can't talk.   Blink your eyes, just to show us that you do understand."   Of course, he blinked them real tight.   Pete smiled, realizing that all he had to do was play the music, and everything ◆ would be fine.

"Without a richer inner life," wrote Hally Wood Stephenson, "no one could have lived through his last illness as Woody did.   He knew it meant death, he knew it meant progressive incapacity.   Still, his gaiety and wit were so inextinguishably

149

a part of him that they survived even when he could no longer speak. I visited him in New Jersey when his motor control was so poor that it took him minutes to light a cigarette. 'I came to see you because I haven't written in so long,' I said. 'With the increase in postage,' he answered, 'it's cheaper to come than write a letter.' We'd been walking in the hospital grounds for a while, my husband limping uncomfortably with a cane and Woody twitching and jerking at every step, but feeling easier when moving. I asked Woody if we couldn't sit down. 'What are we going to do, Hally?' he asked. 'He can't walk and I can't stop and sit down!' "

Until the day of his death—October 3, 1967—Woodrow Wilson Guthrie was as indomitable as the *Darby Ram* of British folklore, and Leadbelly's unbowed and undefeated *Grey Goose:*

> And the knife couldn't stick him
> And the saw couldn't cut him.
> And the last time I seed him, Lord, Lord, Lord,
> He was flying cross the ocean
> With a long string of goslings.
> They was all saying, Quack, Quack.
> Lord, Lord, Lord.

Postscript

WOODY GUTHRIE, PETE SEEGER, CISCO HOUSTON, and many other folk singers returned from World War II, expecting a new era of social justice backed by militant unionism and an active radicalism.

A new organization, People's Songs, was launched, and Woody was passionately involved in its activities. Its publication, the *People's Song Bulletin,* lasted three years, and printed more than 300 songs. *The People's Artist Bureau* was set up to book folk song concerts. In general its policies stemmed from the ideas of the old Almanac days.

However, the scene changed rapidly in a way no one had expected. The labor unions which had inspired and been inspired by Woody and his friends, having won many of their demands, were no longer discontented or militant.

Then came the end of the 40's, bringing the McCarthy Era. Songs of social criticism were still heard but the forbidding cloud of mistrust and conformity tended to stifle their creation and performance. After so many years of Depression and strain, most people were content.

The persecution of leftists and liberals spread like a blight. Even the entertainment world had its blacklist. The Weavers, formed in 1949, were among those barred from television and other communications media.

Despite the blacklist, the Weavers remained the most popular folk song group for over a decade. On the surface they were quite different from the old Almanac Singers; their musical style was polished, their repertory international. They appeared not in the jeans and plaid shirts of the Depression, but in evening clothes. They were heard not in union halls or on picket lines, but in concert halls and night clubs. Nevertheless, their ideals had not changed and their choice of songs proved it.

By the end of the 1950's folk music became big-time entertainment. The Kingston Trio set the style and many groups followed. For the first time, millions of people were listening to American folk songs. True, the arrangements were slick, but many young people would never have become interested in folk music had it not been for the Kingston Trio.

Ever since the end of the Second World War and through the Korean War, a group of young people devoted to grass-roots folk music had made its headquarters at the big fountain in New York's Washington Square Park, the center of Greenwich Village. Sunday mornings banjo pickers and guitar strummers, among them Roger Sprung, John Cohen, Oscar Brand, Jack Elliott, Mary Travers (of Peter, Paul, and Mary), congregated there. They were the heirs of the old Hootenannies, but it was a nonpolitical, song-swapping movement.

From time to time Woody would appear in the Square but his sympathies were not entirely with the newcomers: he found their disassociation from the world around them foreign to him. At a party Woody was asked not to sing political songs. "There are no nonpolitical songs," he replied sharply, and went on to sing the old union songs.

Significant as it was, the grass-roots movement had its limits; it did not relate to contemporary life. In a way, it offered a perfect escape for those who found it easier to live in the dead past than in the clamorous present.

It was the civil rights struggle in the South that ushered in a new era, bringing with it the reappearance of the topical song. Once more folk songs played an important role in the fight for freedom. Many folk singers actively participated, singing on marches, in churches and on picket lines.

A new crop of folk song composers, both black and white, many from comfortable middle class homes, began to write of their direct experiences in the social issues of the time. The new voices included Tom Paxton, Phil Ochs, Eric Anderson, Len Chandler, Mark Spolestra, and Bob Dylan.

It was Woody who most influenced the new topical song writers. Tom Paxton wrote: "The most important thing Woody gave us was courage, the courage to stand up and say the things we believe."

Inspired by Woody's travels, and a desire to escape their own sheltered existence, many performers retraced his footsteps across the country.

The folk singer who could boast of hitchhiking and riding the rails, of sleeping in bedbug-ridden flophouses, of enduring encounters with tobacco-chewing Southern sheriffs and time in flea-bag jails was well on his way to "success." These young people were looking for heroes who *acted* on their principles, as they had in Woody's time.

The person most responsible for the rise and fall of the Topical Song Era was Minnesota-born Bob Dylan, the most important singer-poet since Woody, a voice and conscience for his generation as Woody had been for his own. Who does not know his *Blowin' In The Wind* and *With God On Our Side?*

In the summer of 1964, Dylan created a furor by appearing at the Newport Folk Festival backed by a rock and roll band. The new music, simultaneously booed and applauded by the audience, was called folk-rock, a combination of rock and roll and folk song. Tom Paxton called it "folk-rot" but it started a whole new trend in big-city music; it was musically exciting, and relevant to the mood and temper of the times.

153

By 1964, the topical song movement had out-sung, out-written and out-protested itself.

Dylan's later songs—*Ballad of a Thin Man, Tambourine Man,* and *I Pity the Poor Immigrant*—deal with drugs, the lack of communication between people, the horror of violence, and the need for faith in one's self, much as Woody's songs had done for issues of his own generation.

The world is in ferment, and youth everywhere is searching for a more meaningful life. Woody Guthrie's legacy of love, compassion, brotherhood, and the joy of life, has inspired Dylan and countless others.

"Song to Woody"

Bob Dylan

I'm out here a thousand miles from my home
Walkin' a road of the men who've gone down
I see a new world of people and things
Peter paupers and peasants and princes and kings
Hey, Hey Woody Guthrie! I wrote you a song
About a funny old world that's a comin' along
Seems sick and it's hungry, it's tired and it's torn
It looks like it's a dyin' and it's hardly been born
Hey, Hey Woody Guthrie but I know that you know
All the things that I'm sayin' and many times more
I'm a singin' you this song but I can't sing enough
'Cause there's not many men who've done the things that
    you've done
Here's to Cisco and to Sonny and to Leadbelly too
And to all the good people that traveled with you
Here's to the hearts and hands of the men
That come with the dust and are gone with the wind
I'm leavin' tomorrow but I could leave today
Somewheres down the road someday
The very last thing that I'd want to do
Is to say I been hitting some hard travelin' too.

Discography

Recordings by Woody Guthrie:

Bed on the Floor (Woody Guthrie, Cisco Houston, Sonny Terry). VERVE/FOLKWAYS, FV 9007. Reissued as *Poor Boy.* FOLKWAYS FT 1010.

Bonneville Dam. VERVE/FOLKWAYS FV 9036. Reissued as *This Land Is Your Land.* VERVE/FOLKWAYS FT 1001.

Bound For Glory. FOLKWAYS FA 2481.

Woody Guthrie Sings Folk Songs, Vol. I, (with Cisco Houston, Sonny Terry, Leadbelly, Bess Hawes). FOLKWAYS FA 2483.

Woody Guthrie Sings Folk Songs, Vol. II, (with Sonny Terry, Cisco Houston). FOLKWAYS FA 2484.

Ballads of Sacco and Vanzetti (one song by Pete Seeger). FOLKWAYS FH 5485.

Dust Bowl Ballads (re-issue of 12 of the Victor 78's). FOLKWAYS FH 5212.

Dust Bowl Ballads (same as 5212 plus 2 previously unreleased Victor masters). VICTOR LPV 502.

Library of Congress Recordings. ELEKTRA 271/2. (3 record set)

Songs to Grow On (10"). FOLKWAYS 7015.

Songs to Grow On, Vol. I, (10"). FOLKWAYS 7005.

Hard Travelin' (Cisco Houston, Sonny Terry—includes some Guthrie songs). DISC 110.

Woody Guthrie and Cisco Houston: Folk Songs. STINSON

SLP 44. Re-issued as *Woody Guthrie*. FOLK AR-CHIVE (204) (with 4 additions).

Woody Guthrie and Cisco Houston: More Folk Songs. STINSON SLP 53. Re-issued as *Cisco Houston*. FOLK ARCHIVE (205), (with 4 additions).

The Legendary Woody Guthrie (same as FOLK ARCHIVE 204). TRADITION 2058.

Cowboy Songs sung by Woody Guthrie and Cisco Houston STINSON SLP 32.

Folksay: Volume I and II, (Woody Guthrie, Pete Seeger, Leadbelly, etc.). STINSON SLPX 5.

Folksay: Volume III and IV, (Woody Guthrie, Pete Seeger, Leadbelly, etc.). STINSON SLPX 9.

Folksay: Volume V and VI. STINSON SLPX 12.

Chain Gang (Sonny Terry and Alek Stewart) STINSON SLPX 7. Re-issued as *Sonny Terry* FOLK ARCHIVE 206.

Recordings by the Almanac Singers:

Soil and the Sea (Almanac Singers). MAINSTREAM 56005.

Talking Union and other Union Songs (the Almanac Singers). FOLKWAYS FH 5285 (FP 85-1).

Other recordings of Woody Guthrie songs:

Songs to Grow On (sung by Jack Elliott). FOLKWAYS FC 7501.

Ramblin' Jack Elliott Sings Woody Guthrie and Jimmie Rodgers. MONITOR MFS 380.

Logan English sings the Woody Guthrie Songbag. 20th CENTURY, TFM 3126.

Cisco Houston sings the songs of Woody Guthrie. VAN-GUARD VRS 9089.

Pete Seeger sings Woody Guthrie. FOLKWAYS FTS 31002.

Index

157

The author of numerous books and articles, Henrietta Yurchenco has been Folk Music Editor for *Musical America*
and *The American Record Guide,* and has produced numerous folk music recordings for Folkways, Nonesuch Records,
and the Library of Congress. She has been a pioneer broad-
caster of folk music since 1939. It was in this capacity that
she first met Woody Guthrie, with whom she remained friends
until his death. A member of the State Department's Sub-
committee on Folk Music, Miss Yurchenco is also Professor
of Music Education at the City University of New York.